# STOP
## Sabotaging
## Your Future

## Live the Life
## You Want

**Maxwell Morrison, M.D.**

Addicus Books
Omaha, Nebraska

## An Addicus Nonfiction Book

ISBN: 978-1-950091-77-5
*Typography and cover by Jack Kusler*

This book is not intended to serve as a substitute for a physician. Nor is it the author's intent to give medical advice contrary to that of an attending physician.

## Library of Congress Cataloging-in-Publication Data

Names: Morrison, Maxwell, 1984- author.
Title: Stop sabotaging your future : live the life you want / Maxwell Morrison, M.D.
Description: Omaha, Nebraska : Addicus Books, 2023. I Identifiers: LCCN 2023002267 I ISBN 9781950091775 (trade paperback) Subjects: LCSH: Success. I Self-actualization (Psychology) I Happiness. I BISAC: SELF-HELP / Personal Growth / Happiness I SELF-HELP / Motivational & Inspirational Classification: LCC BF637.S8 M677 2023 I DDC 158.1—dc23/eng/20230131
LC record available at https://lccn.loc.gov/2023002267

Addicus Books, Inc.
P.O. Box 45327
Omaha, Nebraska 68145
AddicusBooks.com
Printed in the United States of America
10 9 8 7 6 5 4 3 2 1

*To my husband, Christian, for his love and support in seeing this book through to its completion.*

# Contents

*Sometimes getting ahead simply starts with getting out of your own way.*

# Introduction

L ife can be wonderful or miserable. The choice is
truly up to you. I am not suggesting that life will
be wonderful *all* the time, but I do hope this book will
help you consider ways to enhance your life. I believe
life is a balance of striving to pursue our goals to the
fullest, and at the same time appreciating all that we
do have. Certainly, we all have problems and emotional
baggage—things we wish were different. Some of these
matters are within our control. Others are not. Whether
you let your current life situation stand in the way of
your happiness is entirely up to you. Happiness is a
choice, based on the actions you take in life. Happiness
does not just merely *happen*.

I am not a psychiatrist; I am an emergency room
physician. However, mental health pervades our lives
and this is never more clear than in the emergency room.
Panic attacks, suicide attempts, self-destructive behaviors
(alcohol/drug abuse, overeating, medication noncompli-
ance, for example), and psychosomatic complaints (complaints for which an organic, nonpsychological cause is
not found) are all too common in the emergency room.
As a result of managing myriad patients for whom mental
health plays a pivotal role in their presentation for care,
I have learned much about the human psyche and the
ensuing disasters that result when it is out of harmony.

My goal is to offer my medical knowledge, along with personal stories and some humor, to guide you on this journey to self-discovery. You may very well be "shooting yourself in the foot" when it comes to finding joy and fulfillment in your life. At times, we truly are our own worst enemies. We all have "demons" and negative thoughts that can creep into our mindset to keep us in a perpetual state of despair. I will offer suggestions on how to break this pattern of self-immolation. I will help you explore the use of tools to put happiness within your reach. I hope to give you bite-sized bits of wisdom, based on life lessons that I have learned, to help you take back your life. We will tackle tough issues such as self-awareness, finding purpose in life, goal setting, and developing a more positive outlook and attitude. I'll also discuss issues such as weight loss, addiction, religion/spirituality, and even financial planning to demonstrate that every aspect of our lives is important to address when it comes to optimizing mental health.

First, I'd like to begin our journey by sharing a little about me. As I mentioned, I am an emergency physician. I have a satisfying career; however, I come from humble beginnings. One of six kids, I came from a working-class family just outside New York City. My parents had to work to make ends meet, and I learned the value of a dollar at a very early age, which is probably why I have such an affnity for clearance sales and happy hours. I waited tables throughout high school, college, and medical school. During that time, I learned a lot about human nature from both the customers and my coworkers. And I learned lessons from the working world that still serve me.

Medicine was never on my radar when I was growing up. I went to college in upstate New York at the State University of New York at Binghamton (Go Bearcats! Wait, what even is a bearcat?!). My degree was in engineering, and although the course of study was difficult, I absolutely loved my college experience. It was during my training as an engineer that I learned the importance of time management and work/life balance. I made many friends with whom I still keep in touch today. In order to pay my own way through college (my parents didn't have "college funds" for all six of us kids), I worked as a secretary and a tutor, whenever I wasn't studying or partying. Binghamton was fantastic, and it taught me how to endure endless winters, how to survive a night out with only ten dollars, and how everyone looked instantly so much more attractive on the two nice days a year when the sun would come out and the sweaters would come off. Yes, college was quite the experience.

I decided to pursue medicine only when I found myself feeling lost during my senior year of college. I had the realization that although, I loved *studying* engineering, I did not actually want to *be* an engineer. It was at that time when my sister Andrea, who was studying nursing at the time, said, "Hey, have you ever thought about becoming a doctor?" At that point, I had thought it was too late because everyone I knew who was pre-med had seemingly decided to take that path from birth. Plus, I'll admit I never really liked pre-med students (no offense to all of my now colleagues!). However, after talking with my sister and doing some research, I realized that becoming a doctor was not an impossibility. In fact, my engineering coursework satisfied many of the prerequisites. Thus, after meeting with my prehealth advisor and watching the first three seasons of *ER* (you know, to really get some field experience), I was set on my new goal of getting into medical school.

As many know, getting into medical school is easier said than done. I had to take two years off to finish my prerequisites, take the MCAT (Medical College Admission Test), and finally apply and interview for medical school. In the interim, I mostly waited tables but also worked as a dental assistant to a kind and very patient dentist (I wasn't very good…). Looking back, while it would have been nice to go straight from college into medical school, those two years were invaluable in my development. I learned so much about how to interact with people working in food service, as well as the basics of patient care as a dental assistant. Moreover, this was the first time I was truly living on my own outside the safety of my parents' nest.

Then the day finally came when I got accepted into medical school. I still can remember the sheer joy of that experience (I believe I even did a cheerleader-style "herkie" upon hearing the news—I nailed it, by the way). So, in the fall of 2008, I started my medical training at the State University of New York at Stony Brook. Medical school certainly was tough, but I think many who undertake it, myself included, look back and describe it as a positive experience. Sure, there was a lot to learn, and there were many, many hours of intense studying, but it was also exhilarating to see yourself grow and become more and more a young professional with each passing month.

The first two years of medical school are regarded as the "didactic years," where there are endless lectures and even more self-study outside the classroom. In the first year, we learned anatomy, neuroanatomy, physiology, and pathology. In the second year, we focused on classes dedicated to each of the organ systems: cardiovascular, gastroenterology, musculoskeletal, and so forth. There was even a class on blood. (I had never even thought of our blood as an "organ," nor did I realize how much there was to know about it!)

Fortunately, although the rigor of the studies was intense, I did feel that my engineering background had prepared me for strenuous coursework, and thus I was able to get through the stressful first two years. What I was *not* prepared for was how much medical school felt like high school. There were only 125 or so students in each class, so it was natural for everyone to know everyone and for gossip to spread like wildfire. Everyone knew who was sleeping with whom, who just broke up, and who failed the most recent exam. It was replete with different cliques of students as well, and we definitely could have labeled the groups with the quintessential titles of jocks (a.k.a. the future orthopedists), nerds, cool kids, and so on. It was absolutely remarkable that although on average we were eight years older than your typical high school student, we could still adopt their social behaviors.

With that said, I was also surprised at how wonderful many of my classmates were and, more importantly, how helpful everyone was. For the most part, people were not cutthroat, nor did they try to push you down to lift themselves up. We all wanted to succeed and see one another graduate. During the last two years of medical school, which is four years total, you embark on your core and elective rotations. This is where you join various teams focused on different specialties. You are on the internal medicine team for two months, then switch over to other core specialties like the pediatrics or obstetrics team the next two months. You can choose some electives along the way, such as emergency medicine, orthopedics, rheumatology, and so on, but you are constantly switching every few weeks to a completely new department.

Although I would love to say this was amazing, mostly it was a matter of trying to learn what you needed to learn and stay out of the way. Sure, there were some cool experiences to be had as a student, but most of the time you were trying to figure out how to be helpful to the residents who were doing the real work without being annoying. At any rate, although improvements could be made in this stint of medical training, it is an invaluable introduction to life in the hospital and an important deciding factor toward our main goal for life after medical school: residency.

Residency is where you choose your medical specialty and learn the nuts and bolts of patient care. Here you go from being an undifferentiated "doctor" to learning how to become an internist, OB-GYN, pediatrician, and the like, depending on the residency you enter. In medical school, you learn the science, the vocabulary, and gain an intense understanding of how the human body works (and when it fails to work).

However, fresh out of medical school, you are virtually a deer in the headlights at the start of your residency. You might understand your patients' diagnoses and problems, as well as what treatments they are undergoing, but you have practically no idea how to actually care for them. Consequently, residency is the process of taking a doe-eyed newbie doctor and turning them into an adept clinician. Residency can be anywhere from three to five or more years, depending on how specialized you wish to become.

I started my emergency medicine residency in 2012 on the upper west side of Manhattan at St. Luke's-Roosevelt Hospital (now a part of the Mount Sinai system). Although I received excellent training, I felt I had traded a part of my humanity for my diploma. We worked many long shifts, and the culture was to work hard and fast to pick up as many patients as you could during a shift, lest you earn the title of the "slow resident." As a result, patients at times started to seem like obstacles to me rather than people. They were a list to churn through and get a disposition for (either admitted to the hospital or discharged home) rather than human beings to heal and comfort. Despite this, my patients were able to teach me so much, including what it means to suffer. In fact, I saw the entire gamut of human suffering, including domestic violence, homelessness, and addiction to drugs and alcohol. In fact, I even found myself at times battling depression and despair.

This is in no way to malign my residency program. In fact, there was much I loved about my residency at St. Luke's-Roosevelt, and the program itself had a reputation for, and prided itself on, taking care of its residents. I believe that my own struggles with mental health during the process were merely the result of trying to learn so much in so little time, compounded by the inherent complexities of learning about flesh-and-blood human beings. The challenges and struggles I faced were the impetus to look for a way out, and ultimately gave me the motivation to write this book.

Fortunately, I did find a way out, and now I want to share with you how you can get out as well. Although I draw from my experiences as a doctor, this book is in no way "just for doctors." My goal is to make this book generalizable to everyone, regardless of their profession or life circumstance. Okay enough about me; let's talk about you. We have a lot to get to, so thanks for picking up this book. Now let's get started!

*Maxwell Morrison, M.D.*

# 1

# Wake-Up Call

*Admitting That You Have a Problem*
*Is a Crucial First Step*

The proverbial "wake-up call" can be one of life's biggest slaps in the face. It's that "oh sh*t" moment, when you finally realize you have troubling emotional issues, simmering just below the surface. We all walk around telling people we're fine, and we think we have it all together. We can put on a good face and go about our daily activities. That is why, generally, wake-up calls almost universally require an external influence— that is, someone or something or an event that tells us we are *not* fine. Only then do we come to the realization that we are not as "fine" as we think. What we do next will determine whether we change our lives for the better or whether we try to ignore what's troubling us and sweep it back under the rug.

I remember the afternoon I received a call from my residency director. "Max, I'm calling because I am worried about you," he said. I was rather shocked by his comment, but I had a feeling I knew what he was talking about. I mean, I *did* just break into tears at our most recent residency retreat. Okay, let me back up. A few weeks earlier we had gone on a retreat for our residency. These retreats were held semiannually and were broken up by class (there were separate retreats for the senior residents as well as the first- and second-year residents). They would sometimes take place at the home of one of the attending physicians (the doctors that supervised us residents) or would involve going to Central Park or hiking. The retreat was a chance to spend a day outside the hospital to connect with our classmates (residents of the same year) and gave us the opportunity to talk more openly about the challenges we face in residency and our lives.

The retreat in question took place at the Garrison Institute, a gorgeous former monastery on the Hudson River, less than an hour north of New York City. I vividly remember the event. After several team-building activities (no, we didn't do "trust falls" into each other's arms, but the activities weren't too far off), we had a session where the fourteen residents in my year (I was a second-year resident at the time) went around in a circle and talked about the challenges we were facing at work. Although part of me wanted to be tough and just roll my eyes at the activity, I decided I would still be tough but actually openly and honestly participate in the activity.

I started speaking about the difficulties I was having with seeing patients as obstacles and not as people, the stress of always feeling like you have to be 100 percent on your game every minute of the day, all the while knowing I was using alcohol to help cope with all this. In essence, I was telling my peers and superiors that I did not like what I was becoming, and before I knew it, I was in tears. My emotions were so powerful that I had to excuse myself and leave. After several minutes, I eventually managed to put on a brave face and get back in the room. The retreat ended shortly after that, and we drove home seemingly to never speak of the incident again.

Now, back to the phone call from my director. I was again taken aback that my cover was blown, that people could see that I wasn't fine despite my insistence to the contrary. I also was a bit surprised that he cared enough to reach out and express his concerns. He could have easily ignored my signs of emotional distress; after all, he was an incredibly busy man with forty-one other residents to supervise, and that was in addition to his own clinical duties. But he was willing to state what I had been willing to bury. I was not happy with my medical residency. The joy and excitement of becoming a full-fledged doctor had quickly eroded under the oppressive demands of actually taking care of patients. Patients had become dehumanized to me, as I focused more and more on getting them out or through the emergency room rather than listening to their stories and empathizing with their feelings.

*Everyone stumbles over the truth from time to time,*
*but most people pick themselves up and hurry off as*
*though nothing has happened.*
—Winston Churchill

I tried to hide my own feelings as well, hurrying through patient encounters to make it through my shifts. After my shifts, I numbed my emotions with excessive alcohol. I told myself that I was just rewarding myself for all my endeavors. *It's not a problem,* I thought. *I work hard and I play hard. What's wrong with that? Besides, most of my senior residents and attending physicians would describe me as a good resident—at least I think they would. (Right, guys?!)* But it took only that simple phone call from my residency director to "pierce" the protective wall I had built up around myself, telling myself everything in my life was fine. In reality, I was surviving, but I was not thriving. I had unresolved emotional issues that were preventing me from being authentically happy with the life I was leading. Something had to change.

Unfortunately, wake-up calls do not tell us *what* we need to change, only that we are *in need* of change. Essentially they are telling us that what we are doing isn't working so well. Look around you. Are there signs that something needs to change in your life? Signs of problems can be rather obvious—you might liken it to a house that's fallen into disrepair. Other signs may be more subtle and can include things such as a sense of uneasiness you can't quite explain or a sinking feeling that a relationship, once a vibrant romance, has begun to decay.

When you stop for introspection, you may notice telltale signs that something is missing in your life. Perhaps it's your spouse asking why you never want to be intimate anymore. If your partner is talking to you about a lack of intimacy, he or she is sending a wake-up call. The next step is to figure out why there is a lack of intimacy. Do you no longer find your partner attractive? Has your relationship become too routine? Do you find yourself being attracted to other potential lovers?

Does your child ask, "Daddy, why are you too tired to play?" Not making time or saving energy for our children can certainly be a red flag. Whatever the case may be, the signs of your despair or unhappiness may not be as hidden as you think. The question again: Are you realistically assessing your life in ways that will help you identify problems so that you can begin to overcome them?

If your supervisor pulls you aside and comments to you about a decline in your work performance, then that's an alarm but not the root of the problem. The next step is to find the cause of the decline. Have you lost interest in your job? Do you have differences with your coworkers? Are other personal problems affecting your ability to concentrate? Whatever the case may be, it is time for careful introspection, but that happens only if we first notice the wake-up call.

Now, a boss or a spouse confronting you is certainly a wake-up call you can't easily ignore. However, more commonly it is the more subtle alarms that hold the keys to our happiness. For example, do you have a sense of dread when going to work each shift? A sense of despair when getting out of bed each day? Do you find yourself irritable around those you love? In my case, it was the

4

latter: I found myself being very short and on edge with those closest to me. It would take me a while to figure out why that was, but I wish I had listened to my own alarms sooner. Had I done so, I could have avoided my next, more direct, wake-up call.

"Is everything all right with you?" my mother asked on the other end of the phone. Again, I was taken aback by her question. "What do you mean?" I replied, knowing full well I had been exposed.

"I don't know," she said, "you seem really on edge and irritable lately. You're just not your normal self."

I was devastated. I care so much about my parents that the idea of them worrying about me was unsettling. I wanted to run or to even try to recover my guise and continue the charade that everything was fine. Deep down, I realized my mother was throwing me a lifeline by bringing up the subject of my unhappiness. I did not know what was wrong with my life, but if my parents had noticed my unhappiness, there must be *something* wrong. I always acted like an optimistic, upbeat person.

Casual onlookers would describe me as successful with a bright future and in the prime of my life. But in the eyes of those closest to me, I was not the person I was pretending to be. Here was my mother alerting me that something was amiss, and as is often the case with mothers, she was right. I was becoming extremely anxious and uneasy, more irritable, and less happy. The alarms were there, and as it turns out, the alarm system was correct. There was in fact a problem, but it would take me a little longer to discover what it was. More on that in an upcoming chapter.

So now it's your turn. Take a few minutes to think about your past week. Think about the interactions you've had with family, friends, and coworkers. Have you sensed that others have noticed a change in you, even if they haven't said so directly? Have your relationships with anyone changed as a result of something deeper going on in your life (even if you can't put your finger on what that "something deeper" is just yet). Are you keeping busy with distractions while neglecting those closest to you? Would your kids rather be playing with you right now? Would your spouse rather be intimate with you right now, but you are choosing to read this book instead? These are the "canaries in the coal mine" that need to be heeded. They are subtle but powerful signs pointing you in the direction of your path to happiness. If you care about your job, your family, your friends, your health, or your life, then you must listen when these canaries tell you something is wrong.

Now, before we continue to delve further, I will add a caveat that not every person who has a sense of despair, uneasiness, or anxiety will benefit from a simple wake-up call. As a physician I do believe that there are some, a select few, people who suffer from what we call pathological anxiety or depression—that is, they have a deeper and possibly even intrinsic neuropsychological abnormality that causes their symptoms, and these people may benefit from medication or professional therapy. If you think this might be you, then please seek professional help from a psychiatrist or therapist.

However, I also believe that many, if not most, people who suffer from anxiety or depression have actual solvable causes for their symptoms. Increasingly in America and the Western world, we are all too quick to throw medications at a problem that merely mask the symptoms rather than tackle the root cause of the problem. We are overmedicated and undertreated. In reality, anxiety and depression are simply some of the many alarms that something is not right with our lives. As I suggested earlier, at this point, you have a choice: You can discover the source of your problems and work to resolve them, or you can forfeit your happiness and choose to be a victim.

# 2

# Stop Lying to Yourself

*Excuses Keep You Trapped*

We all have "white lies" we tell ourselves to get through the day: "I'll go to the gym later," "I'll eat healthy next week," or "My partner and I are just going through a rough patch." Some of these things we tell ourselves are benign, but some are more sinister. There is a difference between lying to ourselves when the intention is there to do the right thing, such as eating right and exercising, and those lies we use to cover up deeper problems such as substance abuse, spousal issues, and problems in our careers.

Lying is a part of human nature, for better or for worse, and in certain ways it is a part of our culture. For example, we may compliment someone's hair style when we actually find it unattractive. Or perhaps we pretend someone's baby is cute when, in reality, we are not sure it's human. In the Western world, there are social norms to uphold, and we are conditioned not to be "impolite" even if it means stretching the truth a little, which, of course, is a euphemism for lying. So, it is little wonder that we have no problem telling these falsehoods to others when we are so adept at lying to ourselves as well.

Imagine a world in which we could say whatever was on our minds and we could be completely honest with ourselves and others. It is so difficult to imagine—it is far from where we are today. I'd imagine politicians, con artists, and snake-oil salesmen would be hit the hardest (given the overlap in the skillset required in those careers...), but nobody would be immune from such a revolution—everyone just saying simply what they thought. In fact, it's an interesting thought exercise to imagine your life without lying. Try this exercise right now. Ask yourself: What toxic relationships would be over without the ability to fake friendship or love? Would you be able to keep your job or be successful in your career? On the positive side, do you think you'd find freedom in your newfound honesty? What if you could tell everyone who you really are, what is truly on your mind, or how you felt? Would you be liberated from no longer having to hide your true self, or would you be mortified by what other people would learn about you?

Would there be potential new friends or relationships that would develop, ones that were no longer hindered by your fears and true feelings? Obviously, this seems the stuff of science fiction, and would not likely ever happen, but it does not mean we can't learn from the exercise. We cannot control whether others lie to us, and as mentioned, given social norms and graces, we cannot always help but lie to others to spare feelings, for instance. The absolute one thing we can control, however, is whether we decide to lie to ourselves.

It was fall of 2016, leaves were changing, there was a crispness in the air, stores were selling pumpkin everything, and the holidays were around the corner. I had recently become engaged to a wonderful woman and had plenty to look forward to as we planned for a wedding. We would spend the rest of our lives together. We were settling into a new house I had bought, and we were raising an adorable labradoodle puppy (adorable, that is, when he wasn't chewing on my shoes or trying to eat all the butter in the house). I had a good job. I was finally finished with residency and seemed to be rocking it as a new ER attending physician. (I hope my coworkers aren't rolling their eyes as they read this.)

I had started a new life in Dallas, Texas, in an attempt to escape the brutal winters of New York City and was enjoying the warm weather and frozen margaritas in January. By all accounts I was successful and seemed to be achieving the "American Dream." (Okay, instead of white picket fences and 2.3 kids, we had a seven-unit townhome and a puppy, but you get the idea.) Yet, something was missing: I wasn't happy, even when on the surface everything seemed great. I wouldn't admit it at the time, though, and in fact, it took me a long time to fully realize my unhappiness; it was far easier to lie to myself and tell myself I was happy, despite many indicators to the contrary.

> *The unexamined life is not worth living.*
> —Socrates

I felt an uneasiness, that despite all the blessings and good things going on in my life, something was keeping me from being happy. I began to tell myself lies in order to be happy, and I ignored several warning signs that should have woken me up much sooner than I did. I started working more, and as a result became increasingly more irritable to my family and fiancée. My use of alcohol increased during my days off and I would lie to myself and saying it was "a reward for how hard I was working," but in hindsight, it seems more that it was used to drown the deeper issues.

Then, the cracks in the facade of my happiness became a chasm because it was becoming clear to me that my relationship with my fiancée was failing. She was a great woman with so much to offer, and we seemed to be such a good fit for each other that it seemed impossible to me that my relationship was no longer "perfect." I could start seeing the imperfections for myself, but was unable to be open and honest about what needed to be

9

done. Instead, I told myself lies. "It will be better after the wedding," "Maybe we need to move back to the Northeast," "Maybe she just needs a new job," or "What if I gave up alcohol?" "Then things will surely improve!" The list goes on and on, and writing about it now brings up a lot of unpleasant memories, but in a twisted way I can't help but laugh at how naïve I was. If only I had the courage to admit and come to terms with the simple truth: I was not in love anymore. The truth finally revealed itself, as it has a way of doing, but I could have saved us months of lost time, heartache, and regret had I been more honest sooner.

Now, although this was my personal story, I do not believe it is in any way unique.

One need look no further than a marriage counseling session or a frank discussion with a divorced person to see that one of the biggest lies we tell ourselves is that "things will be better when...." This applies not only to our relationships with others, but more importantly in our relationship to ourselves. We tell ourselves things are okay even though they are not. Far too often, happiness seems to be at the end of a list of future goals. People convince themselves that the only thing that stands between them and their happiness is a larger salary, a twenty-pound weight loss, a more attractive spouse, a bigger home, more friends, or a faster car. It sounds silly now, but I am sure most, if not all of us, have preconditioned our happiness on such goals.

Fortunately, however, happiness predicated on the attainment of certain goals or new possessions is nothing but a myth, a lie that we humans have perpetuated throughout history. Now, I am not saying that we should not try to better ourselves, or strive to obtain nice things, but when we tie our happiness to those goals and objects, we end up in a cycle of misery. We are unhappy because we don't have something, and one of two things happens: we became more unhappy when we fail to attain a given goal, or if we do obtain our goal, we become unhappy again once we realize that it was not all it's cracked up to be. We continually ask ourselves is there something even better out there that will make me "really" happy. It's time to break that cycle.

The way to start breaking this cycle is to take inventory of your life. As mentioned in the preceding chapter, look for and pay attention to your wake-up calls. Deep down, what is it that you'd like to change? Then, be truly honest about what the problem is and what needs to change. As in my personal example, I continued to lie about what the problem was and the potential solutions. I blamed my failing relationship on everything from our geographic location, to our jobs, to alcohol, and everything in between. But it was only when I could say the words to my fiancée "I don't love you anymore" that positive change could happen. She, naturally, was stunned at first, but with a little time, I think she might too realize the lies present in our relationship. This was a brutally difficult realization to arrive at, and for a long time, months even, I felt guilty and ashamed for hurting her with these lies. Ultimately, however challenging it was to admit the truth, it was of course necessary as starting a marriage based on a foundation of false love surely would not stand.

So, dig deep, be open, and be honest. I encourage you to make a list about what seems to be standing in the way of your happiness. Then, begin analyzing whether or not a given issue is truly making you unhappy or is a symptom of something deeper. For instance, you might decide that your long commute to work is making you unhappy, which of course, it might be (hey, you won't hear me arguing! Working in NYC it used to take me an hour to travel three miles!) But I want you to dig a little deeper and be sure that your unhappiness is not due to your commute to work, rather the mundane job you dread driving to every day. In this case, the commute is the symptom, but the job is the cause. Similarly, you may feel you'll be happier if you lost fifteen pounds, but the real problem might be that you feel your spouse is no longer attracted to you.

Lastly, after you finish the exercise, and find what seems to be problematic in your life, the next step is to start fixing it, *now!* It's time to stop the procrastination and put an end to "mortgaging" your happiness for a later date. Let the simple act of identifying issues in your life and coming up with a plan uplift you. You don't have to wait for the end result to be happy; find joy in knowing that you are in control of your life. You are not a victim, and you have the power to change more than you think you do, even those things that seem outside your control. After you realize this, you will find happiness by being a willing participant rather than a bystander.

Want to lose weight? Great! Start today, and come up with a plan. Do not put it off or proclaim that the "diet starts Monday." If it's important to you, and you think it stands in the way of your happiness, why would you wait? Feel like you are in a dead-end job? Think about what you can do to fix it: Talk to your boss—explore the idea of a promotion or transfer. Learn a new skill online. Research moving to a different part of the country, where you can find more opportunities. Go back to school. Switch companies. There are many possibilities.

Now, this sounds easy to write about, but it's also possible to do, once you stop lying to yourself and making excuses. You might say, "But, I don't have the time," "I don't have the money," "What about my kids?," "I'm too old to make changes," but, if you take a moment to think about these excuses, you can quickly see they are patently ridiculous. You are saying that you don't have the time or the money to be happy? Do your kids not want you to be happy? Are you too old to be happy? Yes, although there are some goals that are more difficult to achieve than others, very few are truly impossible. We use these excuses as a defense mechanism, to protect the status quo. We fear change. But, if you did the exercise correctly, and you honestly believe these goals will increase your happiness, why would you *not* want to change? So, the choice is yours. You can sit and wait for your happiness, and hope that it "happens to you," or you can dig through the lies, throw away the excuses, and work for your happiness today.

# 3

# The Grass Isn't Always Greener

*Stop Comparing Yourself to Others*

We are inundated with images of people living lives we think are better than ours. To admire others, and to be envious, is a part of human nature. Throughout time, mankind has looked with jealous eyes at their neighbors and wondered, "If only I had what they have...." In the past, this was limited to either those immediately around you—family, neighbors, or high-profile people such as tribal leaders or monarchs. Nowadays, thanks to technology, with the mere click of a mouse or flick of a remote control, you have instant access to people from across the globe, both real and fictional, who seem to be just way cooler than you are.

The problem is that envy of others is even more insipid than it used to be. In the past, people glamorized movie stars and politicians as well as athletes and CEOs, just as they do today. In a way, this can be healthy. Having role models can inspire us to be better, to keep improving ourselves, or to even emulate those we admire. Imagine, for example, if more people tried to emulate someone like Mother Teresa, arguably the world would be a better place. But today, we are in a state of information overload. Fifty years ago, you had only a handful of television channels, and otherwise you saw celebrities only in print media, heard them on the radio, or saw them on television. Now, we have channels upon channels and an infinite number of websites devoted to the lifestyles of the elite. You could spend every waking moment following the lives of other people, while simultaneously neglecting your own.

About fifteen years ago, the problem deepened with the advent of social media. What was once hailed as a novel way for people to stay connected has, in my view, become a pitfall for perpetuating despair. It started with a social networking service, MySpace, followed by Facebook, Twitter, Instagram, and Snapchat, among others. Don't get me wrong, I am not against social media; in fact, I even had a Facebook account at one point. I am simply saying that the many benefits and entertainment derived from these platforms can be outweighed by the misery they may cause if misused.

As an example, let's say you are feeling a little lonely, so you decide to log onto Facebook and see what all your "friends" are up to. Within an instant, you are reading posts from people, some of whom you barely know, who appear to be having so much more fun than you are. Looks like Sally had another baby ("Hmmm...I don't have any kids yet," you think to yourself), Mike had a blast at his birthday party ("Looks like everyone else was invited, except me," you lament). And your friend Becky posted yet another picture of her and her new boyfriend (of like two weeks) with a nauseating hashtag such as #feelingblessed.

That's not even mentioning all the posts in which people are ruining a season finale you were waiting to see. At times, it seems people somehow feel as though having a Facebook account qualifies them as a political pundit or foreign policy expert. So, instead of feeling up-lifted, you now are anywhere from depressed to irritated, and you decide to cheer yourself up with a bowl of ice cream and a little TV. You turn on the TV and are now subjected to deciding whether you should *Keep Up with the Kardashians,* watch an episode of *Fixer Upper* (noting that everyone seems to have a nicer house than you), or catch up on your favorite sitcom (in which everybody is gorgeous and can afford lavish living arrangements in a big city without ever seeming to have to work).

Now that you feel you've hit rock bottom, you settle on watching *The Biggest Loser* because hey, at least you're not *them!*

Okay, perhaps my assessment is a pessimistic view of modern media, and of course a bit of a hyperbole, but I wish to illustrate a point. There is limitless entertainment in the modern world, but without a little perspective it can quickly and easily make your world seem pretty dull. Take Snapchat, for instance, where you can easily keep up with those closest to you through their photos, which is great for people you might not see too often, or for your friend who is on their honeymoon (provided she uses some discretion with the photos she posts).

However, humans are, to varying degrees, envious by nature, and even the best of us can fall prey to being envious of others or feeling our lives pale in comparison. We generally see posts of people at their best, during the highlights of their lives. What they don't post are all the drudgery and doldrums of their daily lives that we all experience: arguments with our partners, lugging bags to the airport, or other mundane activities that went into creating that picture-perfect moment. Because of this, it's easy to forget that other people experience hardship too, and we start to adopt a victim mentality. We begin to think, "If only I had what *they* have, then I would be happy" or "Other people have it so easy; why can't I be as lucky as *they* are?" The notion begins to ingrain itself into us that some people are fortunate and others are not. We then start to believe we fall into the latter group.

The main problem with social media posts is that they often emphasize the exciting things—the graduations, birth announcements, weddings, and work promotions. We are quick to forget that there was a process that led to those celebrations.

A friend may not stop posting about having finally found the "man of her dreams," but we didn't see or hear about all the creeps, weirdos, and losers she had to sort through to find him. (Trust me, they're out there.) Another friend may seem to carry on and on about her new baby girl, or her "little blessing," as she calls her, but you might not know about the miscarriages or trouble she had conceiving.

*If you look really closely,*
*most overnight successes took a long time.*
—Steve Jobs

Lastly, that photo of your friend's seemingly awesome vacation in Costa Rica neglected to mention the overtime shifts he had to put in to be able to afford the trip, or the "Montezuma's Revenge" he came home with as a "souvenir." The point is that snapshots are just that: moments in time of a particular event. They tell us nothing of what happened before or what happened after. Obviously, we don't wish hardships on our friends and family (otherwise, that would make us horrible people), but we need to realize that there is more to the picture than what appears on our computer screens. By doing so, we can start to actually feel happy for others, but more importantly, we can start feeling happy about ourselves.

Television and social media are not the only lenses through which we compare ourselves to others. We do so all the time in real life as well. Think about how many times you were at the gym and thought about the person next to you, *Why can't I look like that?* Or perhaps you wonder why your friend has such a nicer car than you. The list can go on and on. Such comparisons can motivate us to improve ourselves, but there is a greater likelihood that we make ourselves miserable with such comparisons. The problem arises when the concept of trying to improve ourselves slowly convinces us that we are not happy with what we have. We focus on what's missing rather than what is present. Regardless of whether it's a killer beach body, a fast car, or a mansion of a home, we begin to fall into the trap of "I'd be happy if...," and we start to make our happiness dependent on arbitrary objectives. Worse, still, is that we let *other* people create those objectives for us. You might not have even cared that you drove a clunker of a car, until your neighbor pulled up in their new Maserati. This happens on so many levels and can be quite toxic to our well-being.

You also might not even realize that this is happening. For instance, you and your friend go on a double date, and you automatically start to wonder why your partner can't be as attractive and humorous as their partner. Before the date, you didn't think there was any problem with your partner, but *now* it comes to mind, and the entire way home you are trying to remember your login information for your online dating profile. Suddenly, your comparisons go from being productive to destructive.

Speaking of dating, let's look at online dating. I can say that I personally have fallen prey to the limitless comparisons that the Internet provides. I doubt I am alone when saying that while on a date with someone I've contemplated making plans to do something with someone else whose online profile seemed more interesting than my companion at the time. Before you look at me disapprovingly, please know I felt a little guilty about such thoughts that floated through my mind. This example, however, reminds me that we face a seemingly infinite array of choices in the dating pool. It makes focusing on one person difficult, when there appears to be endless other options just a click or swipe away. No wonder marital rates are on the decline now that it's easier than ever to play the field.

Again, I am not against competition, and I think that comparison can be a useful tool when used productively. However, once you let it consume you to the point of dwelling on what you don't have as opposed to what you do have, that's when it becomes the prime ingredient for misery.

The choice is yours as to what you will do when you find yourself comparing your life to that of others. Instead of letting such comparisons commandeer your happiness, turn this pattern of thinking into something productive. Do you want a nicer car, one like the neighbor has? Come up with a plan to achieve your goal. Is it worth cutting back on other expenses like nights out at a restaurant or buying new clothes every season to achieve your goal of buying a new car? If so, go for it. If not, you are starting to realize that maybe there are other things you value more than a new car.

Furthermore, don't forget about all you *do* have— things that are far more valuable than a car or other consumer goods. Maybe you have a job you love, a supportive and loving spouse or partner, you have wonderful kids, or are in good health. Bottom line, when we start to focus on what we lack, it's a wake-up call to take inventory of all we do have. What is it that you are grateful for? Gratitude chases away feelings of envy and loneliness.

In summary, be aware that we tend to look at one feature of other people's lives and then generalize about their whole life. As a result, it is no surprise that studies show that social media use is associated with higher rates of depression and anxiety. Remember, what you see on social media is merely a "snapshot in time" of someone else's life. All the while we pay no attention to the struggles that people may have had to make to get what they have or to reach where they are. We assume it was handed to them. Just remember that no one is perfect. Everyone has challenges.

We all have hardships and obstacles to overcome, and what seems glamorous on the outside may be hell behind closed doors. Instead of playing the victim, and letting your happiness slip away from you, use your emotions productively and be grateful for all you do have.

# 4

# Set Goals for Yourself

*If You Don't Plan, You May Accept Anything*
*That Comes Your Way*

Most of us think about and plan for the future.
As a species, we are always interested in what's
next. Early man had to continually plan for the future:
where the wild game would be migrating next, what
crops could they expect this year, where was the best
place to build shelter. It is this industriousness that has
allowed us to flourish and become the dominant species
on Earth. Still, just as humans did hundreds of years ago,
we still need to plan where our next meal is coming
from or where we are going to live.

In most industrial societies, these basic needs are
met more easily than they were for prehistoric man, yet
our desire to plan and look to the future still burns within
us. Instead of focusing on food and shelter, we begin
to dream, obsess, and agonize over other concerns:
planning a wedding, getting a new job, finishing school,
or starting a family. Although sometimes planning can be
fun, and other times stressful, its most salient feature is
that it makes us feels alive. It gives us hope—something
to which to look forward.

Unsurprisingly, many people who fall into depression do so because they have lost a sense of purpose:
they have no goals for themselves. In fact, just the other
night at work I had the sad case of a young patient in

her early twenties who tried to take her own life by overdosing on her antidepressants. When I asked her what triggered her impulse to act in such a way, she responded by saying that she simply felt she had nothing to live for.

Fortunately, drug manufacturers have made antidepressants way safer than they used to be (having finally realized that depressed people are the ones most likely to attempt suicide). The patient ended up improving after some observation and supportive care. She was transferred to a psychiatric facility for further treatment. Still, as with most things, an ounce of prevention is worth a pound of cure, so let's explore what ignited her impulse for suicide in the first place.

One of the more common things I hear from suicidal patients in the emergency room is some variant of "I have nothing to live for." They then cite how their spouse left them, they lost their job, they don't see their kids, or a parent died. None of us are exempt from such emotionally painful experiences. Some people, like the young lady in the emergency room, have given up hope for the future and have stopped planning for it. Without plans for a better tomorrow, they no longer feel that life is worth living today.

Suicidal patients are the extreme end of this spectrum, but think about your life and when you felt most alive. Likely your memory will conjure up events such as a wedding, training for or completing a marathon, finishing high school or an advanced degree, or having a child. These are all events that took time to complete, with all the anticipation and excitement leading up to them. And although there was likely a lot of stress peppered in with the joy and excitement, these events probably gave you a sense of purpose and, more importantly, a sense that you were planning a bright future.

Ironically, these same events that inspired our sense of purpose when we were working toward them can also be a source of depression after the goal is achieved. Conditions such as postpartum depression are a well-documented examples of this phenomenon. In fact, a recent article in the Annals of General Psychiatry estimates the prevalence of postpartum depression to be 10 to 15 percent in the United States.

Similarly, we have all seen marriages fall by the wayside after the "honeymoon phase" is over, but why is that? Well, as mentioned in chapter 2, part of the problem is that we think that these events will transform us. We think our partner will start behaving better "after the wedding" or that we will be a perpetually "healthy person" after having completed a marathon and the training has stopped. However, a larger issue, and one that this chapter addresses, is that after these events are over we lose a huge motivating force in our lives. Unless we again start planning for the future, depression and anxiety may set in.

Surprisingly, even seemingly successful people are not immune to feelings of depression and hopelessness that arise after having gotten "everything they ever dreamed of." It seems you don't have to look too hard to find a celebrity suicide, a movie star in drug rehab, or a music star whose marriage is on the rocks. The very same celebrities who seem to have it all, more than we could ever dream of, are vulnerable to the same psychological infirmities as the rest of us. Despite being idolized, worshipped, and revered, even the loftiest stars can suffer. In reality, the theme is the same—after you stop dreaming, you're vulnerable to depression.

If movie stars and athletes are not immune from such feelings, then it can certainly happen to far more ordinary people. I consider myself among this group. By all accounts, I was what most people would probably consider successful. I worked my way through high school and college, got into medical school, and even continued waiting tables during my medical training. I was accepted into a respected residency program and graduated three years later with a good job in a new state, and a beautiful woman, the girlfriend who would then become my fiancée.

However, something still felt like it was missing. After all my hard work, all my training, there was a feeling of, "That's it?" I wracked my brain as I pondered, "What's next?" I had reached my goal, climbed my mountain, only to discover emptiness on the other side. After all my determination, years of delayed gratification, and surviving the gauntlet of medical education, I found myself staring at a future of thirty to forty years of what seemed like "just another job." There were no more graduations, no more spring breaks or final exams, just the routine of showing up to work on time, doing my job, and then going home. Where had all the excitement gone? It seemed like there was nothing left to look forward to except maybe a retirement somewhere down the line with all-I-can-eat Jell-O. Don't get me wrong, I wasn't miserable. I love my job and am proud of what we doctors, nurses, techs, and ancillary staff do in health care. But the journey I had taken just all seemed anticlimactic. I struggled with where my life was going and what was next for me and my career. I lacked goals, not because there wasn't anything left to achieve, but more because I was used to having "carrots" dangled in front of me.

The past dozen or so years of my life were fed by a list of goals. I believed that if I simply kept achieving, I would reach the next milestone. From passing the MCAT (Medical College Admission Test) to getting into medical school, and finally getting my Doctorate of Medicine degree, it seemed that I wouldn't ever have to wait much more than a few months for a new milestone to have been met. Each achievement brought with it a dopamine surge to keep me elated and ready to move on to the next challenge. But, then, it all stopped, and I had to start to look for new goals and sources of motivation.

My story is certainly not unique, and although I used graduate school as an example, everyone has their own goals. For some, it could be their lifelong dream to get married and have children. After that's done, and the kids are grown up, they may begin to wonder what the purpose of their life is now. Another could be the journey you went through to scrimp and save so you could finally buy that house you always wanted, but after you accomplish that, you may ask yourself, "Now what do I do?" Any of us can feel a letdown after attaining things for which we worked hard. I will even admit I've felt down after finishing a series on Netflix. Sure, the series had a great ending, but now what do I do without a new episode to which to look forward? Regardless of your situation, the point is that oftentimes the journey to your dream can feel more fulfilling than the dream itself. Thus, when we stop dreaming or stop reaching for our goals, loneliness, depression, and emptiness can set in.

> *Well done is better than well said.*
> —Benjamin Franklin

So, what's the solution? Well, simply put, continue dreaming. Okay, that's a little vague, but the concept is actually simple. Although some of the dreams of our past may seem difcult to top, there are countless other joys for which we can be grateful. For example, the joy of having a family of your own or finally getting that promotion certainly are momentous occasions; the truth is that the mere presence of a goal or dream, and not necessarily its grandeur or magnitude, can keep you happy. Although I certainly encourage people to dream big, when it comes to their goals, the size is not important. By simply setting goals for yourself, you continue to tap into that innate human desire to plan for the future and also create a life, rich with experiences.

There are so many things that can fill this need that it's a wonder people ever say they have problems deciding on goals. Some common and attainable goals for most people include:

- Setting fitness goals (running a 5k or a marathon, going to the gym three times a week, losing weight)
- Exploring a new hobby (taking up crafts, learning to play tennis, reading)
- Learning a new language or skill
- Traveling to a new destination
- Paying off debts, credit cards, mortgage
- Remodeling the house
- Making a point to make new friends or connections
- Finding a new partner (meeting new people, online dating)
- Changing bad habits (drinking, gambling, smoking)
- Making time for family and friends (Sunday dinners, lunch get-togethers, family night)

There, I came up with this list of ten things in less than five minutes, so certainly you can do the same. Look over my list again. I am sure you can find at least a variation of one of these things that sparks an idea for you. The most important part when establishing a new goal is to make sure it's meaningful—that is important to you. Setting goals does not have to be a complex process, and in fact can be done quite easily. I would encourage you to decide on two or three goals. Next, write a plan for *how* you would achieve the goal and then, why that goal is important to you. I cannot emphasize this enough, as simple as it sounds. If you cannot come up with a plan to execute your goal, or standards by which success is to be measured, then your goal will seem too nebulous and fail to inspire you.

For instance, let's take a common goal: weight loss. There is a huge difference between Person A, who says, "I want to lose weight by May of this year," and Person B who says, more specifically, "I want to lose 30 pounds by May of this year. I plan to give up refined carbohydrates, do 30 minutes of cardio four times a week, with an average goal rate of weight loss of 1.5 pounds per week, for the next 20 weeks." Now, who do you think is more likely to succeed in their weight loss goal? Person A or Person B? Obviously, Person B seems determined and has a goal clearly outlined. I encourage you to have both short- and long-term goals; they can be big or small goals. Regardless, you must have a plan outlined for your goals.

Take as another example the case of someone who wants to be a movie star, like pretty much every bartender in Manhattan. This is a great goal, but what's the plan? Are you going to simply wait tables and hope to get "discovered," or are you going to take acting classes, audition for parts, create headshots for your portfolio, and network with producers? (Just make sure you stay off the casting couch!) Plans are paramount to success, and you are more likely to get from point A to point B if you have a map. After creating a plan, ask a mentor or trusted friend to review the plan—perhaps they can help you put things into focus. Plans also need to be flexible, and they may require adjustment as you pursue your goals. Ideally, finding someone or even researching someone who did something like what you want to do can give you valuable insights. They allow you to learn from their experience. Now, I am not saying that you cannot accomplish your goals without a mentor, but why reinvent the wheel if you don't have to. Educating yourself is important.

Now, the second part of the goal-setting process, and in my view, just as important, is the reasoning behind your goal. The stronger the reason, the better your chances of success. Some reasons can be quite compelling. For instance, someone whose goal it is to get their debt under control may cite the reason as being "so my lender doesn't foreclose on my house" or "so my car doesn't get repossessed." Certainly, these are strong motivating forces.

However, some reasons can also be a little more fun or light-hearted, such as the goal of learning a new hobby or learning to play an instrument. Maybe you want to take up knitting so you can knit blankets for your friends, or you simply like the way an instrument sounds. These activities, albeit hobbies, can be most rewarding. Although these might seem like less compelling reasons, if you are interested enough in the endeavor they could be enough to motivate you toward accomplishment.

Keep in mind, however, that just as when you were describing your goals, the more specific you can be about your motivations, the more powerful they are. Let's take another look at Person A and Person B, both of whom were trying to lose weight. When asked why they want to lose weight, Person A might respond, "Because I want to look good" or "I want to feel better." Noble as these reasons are, a little more specificity would go a long way in fueling the drive to achieve these goals. Now, on the other hand, Person B might respond, "So I can fit into my old work clothes" or "To get off my blood pressure or diabetes medications." These goals are far more tangible than merely looking or feeling better. They demonstrate immediate consequences for Person B, and therefore will be far more motivating.

As for me, I found I was able to create new goals after having graduated residency, which at the time had me feeling like there was nowhere to go but down. So, I resolved to create new goals such as paying my student debt off, buying a house, traveling to one new place a year, and starting to date again. My reasons were strong enough to compel me toward completing these goals. I *hate* being in debt, so I wanted my loans paid off for the sense of freedom that comes with being debt-free. I wanted to buy a house to be a property owner and build equity as part of my financial portfolio. I want to see the world, and I know without forcing myself to a goal of traveling I could easily let months and years slip by without ever going anywhere. Lastly, after my break-up with my fiancée, I knew I needed to start dating again if I didn't want to end up being alone. I'd have to start putting myself back out there. My reasons might be different from yours if you have goals similar to mine, but as long as they are compelling enough to motivate you, then that's all that matters.

In summary, on some level, we all live, think, and plan for the future. When we start to feel that we have no plans or goals, we start to think that we have no future. Depression, emptiness, and despair are not far behind at that point. The solution is simpler than we think, but we must start planning, creating goals, and stirring up passions.

Goals can range from the minute to the mega, but as long as they have meaning to you, they will do the trick of restoring that sense of purpose in your life. So, start thinking of some potential goals, contemplate their significance to you, and then develop a plan. The more meaningful the goal and the more in-depth the plan, the more likely you are to succeed. Start today and don't let your past accomplishments, or failures, get in the way of your future!

# 5

# Don't Take "No" for an Answer

*Stop Telling Yourself "You Can't"*

It's remarkable to ponder how much we let ourselves stand in the way of our own happiness. Stop for a minute and see if any of these phrases sound familiar: "I don't have time to exercise," "I can't afford a vacation," "I'll never find the right person," "I won't get picked for the promotion." I could go on with such a list, but you get the point. We tell ourselves negative, self-defeating phrases like this, and the result is: We give ourselves permission to not try. We call the game before it even started. This is so common because it's so easy. If we believe something is impossible, then we save ourselves the work of trying and remove the risk of failing. We don't gain anything when our goal is to simply protect ourselves from loss.

It is natural for humans to seek safety and avoid loss. When we put ourselves "out on a ledge," there's a chance we'll fall, so the reward realized must be much greater than the perceived risk in order for us to take a chance. In fact, this phenomenon is known as *loss aversion* and has been well characterized by preeminent psychologists Daniel Kahneman and Amos Tversky. Their scientific work has demonstrated that we are much more upset about losing $5.00 than we would be happy to gain $5.00. Although it is somewhat counterintuitive, years of evolution have fostered this mindset within us. This is an adaptive behavior that has its merits—in "healthy doses," it prevents us from overly risky behavior that might decrease our chances of survival.

At the same time, however, fear or negative self-talk can get in the way of accomplishing goals and leading fulfilling lives. In reality, negative views such as these serve two purposes: they conveniently excuse us from having to do the hard work of bettering ourselves, all the while reinforcing a vision of ourselves as victims. It is much easier to say "woe is me" than to change our current situation.

However, if we don't take risks, if we don't make changes, then perhaps our lives won't get any worse, but they definitely won't get any better. So it's time to break this negative mindset and start accomplishing what you thought you never could. I'd like to introduce what I call the "Non-Negotiable Plan." The first step is to focus on what it is you think you can't do, and then analyze what is standing in your way of doing it. We humans have an incredible ability to rationalize our behaviors, such that coming up with this list should be relatively easy. For instance, in the case of the person who says that they "don't have time to exercise," the excuses can range from "I work too much," "I'm too tired," "I don't know how or what to do."

Next, you need to decide how important this goal is to you. How would your life be better if you *did* exercise? Would you lose weight, build muscle, have more confidence, enjoy better health and perhaps need to take fewer medications? These, to me, all seem like worthy benefits, so much so that it would be worth finding time to exercise. This step cannot be overstated: if you want to change your behavior, you have to find reasons that are worthwhile to make the change.

## The Non-Negotiable Plan

- Identify what it is you *can't* do.
- Analyze your reasons *why* you cannot do it.
- Identify what it is you *can* do.
- Make your plan non-negotiable

After you have a goal, have analyzed your prior excuses, and have come up with reasons why accomplishing this goal would be important, the next step is to eliminate your excuses by coming up with a manageable plan and making it non-negotiable. You say you don't have time to work out? Well, maybe you don't have 30 minutes, but maybe you have 20. Maybe you only have 15 minutes, or 10, or 5, it doesn't really matter.

The point is that you have decided this goal is worth doing, which means there must be *some* amount of time you deem worthy of devoting to it. Furthermore, you might think that five minutes of exercise a day is not going to yield much in the way of results, but it definitely is better than zero minutes of exercise. At this stage, the time is not as important as finding a commitment you can and will stick with.

We all have our own stories, and the stories of friends or family with lofty champagne-fueled New Year's resolutions such as "I can *totally* climb Mount Everest." Invariably, we fail at these goals by February (turns out Mount Everest is *really* tall). Buoyed by the gluttony of the holidays, we come up with extreme goals to take control of our lives by committing to exercise "30 minutes every day," "giving up carbs," "not eating any food that casts a shadow." Okay, I made that last one up, but you can insert whatever new trend or latest fad is popular. Sooner or later, life gets in the way, and we realize that our goal was not sustainable. Disheartened, we abandon our resolutions with an all-or-nothing attitude and wait until next year to repeat the process.

What I have learned, having had this experience myself, is that we need to abandon the idea of all-or-nothing, and sometimes we need to settle for something practical. So, your plan to exercise thirty minutes every day didn't pan out? Well, don't give up entirely! What about fifteen minutes every day, or fifteen minutes five days a week? Whatever the time frame is here is not nearly as important as long as it is something you can make non-negotiable. What I mean by that is that you need to pick something that you will stick to, no matter what, no excuses.

Maybe you can't commit to running three miles three times a week, but what about one or two miles two times a week? All too often we have a mindset of "go big or go home" that we forget that even modest amounts of exercise can make a difference. As a physician, I can attest that even moderate amounts of weight loss (5–10 percent of total body weight) or exercise can decrease our resting blood pressure and decrease the risk for diabetes and stroke. Maybe walking around the block a few times is all you can commit to right now, but it's better than not doing it at all.

No change is too small at this point, and truly any positive change you make is better than nothing. The secret is that after you find something you can commit to, and you actually commit to it, more often than not you create a positive habit that has a snowball effect. When you realize you can dedicate five minutes a day to exercise, you will find it's easier to start dedicating six, eight, maybe even ten minutes a day. It has become a habit, a non-negotiable, that you somehow seem to make time for, despite the fact that not too long ago you thought you "didn't have any time" at all for it.

As for finding the time, if you make the change small enough, you can certainly find some point in a twenty-four-hour day where you can achieve your goal, especially if you are starting at five or ten minutes. Of course, you could wake up a little earlier, or go to bed a little later, but with a little creativity you can avoid having to adjust your sleep schedule. I've seen nurses speed walking in the halls on their breaks. I've heard of people doing squats, push-ups, or crunches while on hold during a phone call. I personally have even done push-ups or walked up and down steps during a break. (I can only imagine what my nurses think at work when I come back from the "bathroom" all red in the face and out of breath!)

So, right, maybe you don't have thirty minutes at a time to exercise, but we all have short breaks throughout the day. In order to squeeze in activity, you simply must be creative. Take a set of weights or an exercise mat to work, if your office space allows. Find where the stairs are, or where the long hallways are that would make an effective track. Maybe there's a gym nearby that you can get to on your lunch break or a park outside? Whatever the case, the trick is to make it convenient, make it easy and non-negotiable, so that you have no excuse for not following through. Yes, thirty minutes is a lot of time all at once for many people, but virtually anyone can find six five-minute blocks of time in their day.

As a personal example, I have always believed in physical fitness (not that you would always know it by looking at me), but I found it difficult to work exercise into my routine as a busy resident living in a small New York City apartment. I joined one of those chain gyms close by, but I would have to wait for the right times to go when it wasn't too crowded. Even then, time was a challenge. I had to walk ten minutes each way to get there, then I had to change clothes at the gym, only to wait for machines or weights. I had to change back into my street clothes, feeling sweaty. My forty-five-minute workout turned into an hour-and-a-half ordeal (okay, perhaps ordeal is a bit dramatic). Sure enough, the excuses would come all too easily in order to not endure this hardship. I certainly didn't have the time, energy, or willpower to keep up with that ritual during my residency.

I came to the realization that even doing a less intense workout in my home would be better than no workout at all. I knew I wasn't going to get "ripped" with what I could do at home, but I certainly wasn't going to make any physical improvements by talking myself out of going to the gym time and again. So, I invested in one pair of thirty-five-pound dumbbells and came up with a quick routine I could do in twenty to twenty-five minutes (usually while watching an episode of *Seinfeld* or *Frasier*).

> *It does not matter how slowly you go*
> *so long as you do not stop.*
> —Confucius

I decided that I would make this non-negotiable and perform this routine every three days. Sure enough, it worked. I relished how quickly the routine was done, and moreover how much time I saved by not having to go to the gym. It wasn't perfect. I had to temporarily rearrange some furniture, which in an NYC apartment meant piling the living room table on top of the couch and waiting until my roommate wasn't around (which because he was a general surgery resident, was often). Sometimes I forced myself to wake up early or go to bed later to get it done. However, because it was so convenient, it felt easier to do. I was probably never going to make it on the cover of *Men's Fitness* magazine with this routine, but I was able to maintain my weight during residency and stay fit, so for me, that was a win.

Most of this chapter has focused on fitness goals or challenges, mostly because they are easily relatable, but also because they nicely demonstrate my non-negotiable method. We can adapt this strategy just as easily to other facets of our lives where we tell ourselves "we can't."

Whether it is taking that vacation we "can't aford," or paying off that debt we "can't get out of," after you apply the right methods, you'll start to realize all you can do. Right, maybe you can't afford a $3,000 trip to Hawaii this year, but what about a $1,000 trip to the Bahamas? Instead of giving up altogether, what about saving up for the trip next year?

Perhaps $3,000 seems daunting to you, but what if you think about saving $250 a month for a year. Does that seem more palatable? You would need to save only $125 a month if you put the trip off for two years. Then of course there's the option of researching deals for flights and hotels, or finding friends to help share expenses.

The point is, if you have a goal or a dream, making it happen is not nearly as far-fetched as you might think. I am all for being grounded in reality, but as you can see, with a focused, detailed plan, you can keep your dreams firmly rooted in reality. The trick is, once again, to think big and then break it down into manageable steps that you can, and will, do.

Now, it's time for you to think about some goals you've had that might never have seemed possible. Start dreaming big and remember the Non-Negotiable Plan: Dig deep to find out what goal you've always thought you *can't* do, uncover the reasons you've told yourself why not, come up with a list of things you *can do* to get to that goal, and then make them non-negotiable. Your future is waiting.

# 6

# Time for a Change

*Stop Shooting Yourself in the Foot*

Insanity is often defined as doing the same thing over and over again and expecting different results. Most people would agree that this definition of insanity is valid, yet many of us do exactly that. We lament our lives but refuse to change. We accept the status quo because to do something about it requires energy. It's simply easier to whine than to win. Furthermore, the negative effects of our inaction are compounded when our behaviors are not conducive to good health—overeating, binge drinking, or compulsive spending. These types of behaviors not only fail to improve our lives, but they are also likely the cause of our miseries.

To illustrate the theme of this chapter, let's discuss alcohol use as it is both common and ripe for abuse. "I'm never drinking again!" is a common refrain among both novice drinkers and seasoned alcoholics alike after a particularly heavy night of drinking. What separates the two is that the former will likely learn from their mistakes, while the latter fails to examine the problem. Still, there are many among us who would not identify as alcoholics but certainly fall into destructive patterns regarding alcohol. I'll give you an example, and who better to use than myself.

I had grown up around alcohol my whole life, and drinking was definitely perceived as normal. My family and virtually all of my friends generally enjoy imbibing, making it easy to enjoy a drink any day of the week. My first jobs were in the food service industry, where sneaking drinks on the job is essentially part of your pay. Fortunately, all of the people in my life are hardworking and successful, but this made it difficult for me to see that just because I wasn't on skid row didn't mean I had a healthy relationship with alcohol.

I started to notice a pattern of alcohol abuse during my residency. In stressful situations and after long hours caring for patients, I felt a need for an emotional release. I suppose I was disenchanted to learn that my life wouldn't just be one big episode of *Grey's Anatomy* either. As a result of these stressors and because I was so comfortable with alcohol (at least it was not heroin, right?!), I had gotten into a habit of drinking fairly heavily on my time off. In my medical residency, we were blessed to get two weekends off per month, and I was sure to use them to the fullest. Friday night would kick off with a happy hour, and because in NYC there are numerous bars on every street, the party could easily extend into the wee hours of the morning. (Bars closed at 4.00 A.M. in New York!)

Staying out late was fun, and it allowed me to maximize my alcohol consumption. Saturday mornings, however, were less fun, and any attempts to be productive were certainly painfully labored. It became an easy decision to cut off any productive work early and "drunkersize" my weekend starting with an all-you-can-drink brunch (which were also plentiful in New York City). Not wanting to stop the party there, Saturday would then progress to a brewery, cocktails at home with friends, or some other party that was going on. Once again, the night could go late until I would eventually make it home.

Sundays were very much the same, although I somehow always managed to peel myself out of a bed for Mass like a good little Catholic boy. But Sundays were essentially a rinse and repeat of Saturdays, searching for any way to alleviate my hangover in a socially acceptable way ("Real alcoholics don't drink mimosas!" I told myself).

Thankfully, better judgment would often, but not always, eventually take over slowing down the alcohol consumption in preparation for a return to reality on Monday morning. Sunday nights, however, could be unpleasant, tossing and turning as my body and mind suffered the unpleasant effects of alcohol withdrawal. Excessive sweating, tremors, and racing thoughts, coupled with anxiety for the week ahead, made sleep difficult, if not impossible. Thankfully, morning would come, and I would pull myself together enough to make it to work, even if one would describe me as neither bright-eyed nor bushy-tailed.

I would always eventually get back into the groove at work despite a sluggish start to the work week. I noticed, however, that I was somewhat irritable, quiet, and reserved after my drinking benders. Quite frankly, I would feel like a shell of my actual self. Things would bother me that normally wouldn't, and work seemed to take longer to complete. Fortunately, as the work week went on, I would return back to my normal self, ready to handle the stress of work and medical training. However, my behavior became a vicious cycle. While back to work, I was grateful to feel my normal self, and having to go to work was a strong impetus to stay sober, but then, the stressors of work would quickly compel me to once again search for a release. Sure enough, once I had another day or two off it was back to the bottle or nearest bar to get the party started again. You can pretty much guess how the rest of the story for the weekend goes.

Although I was functioning from the outside looking in, I clearly was not thriving. Worse still, in this case, I thought alcohol was the solution to the stress of my work, but it was, in fact, the cause of my problem. This is the quintessential vicious cycle that can derail our lives. I drank because I was stressed, but drinking actually perpetuated my stress in the form of sleepless nights and anxiety. Another main issue was that because I was "functioning," I couldn't see the problem clearly. I showed up to work on time, performed well, and never called in sick. Thus I never suffered any external punishments that might have forced me to realize the gravity of my problem. I had to really undergo some harsh introspection to decide that I needed to change my relationship with alcohol.

Now you might drink only occasionally, or not drink at all, but you can substitute many other vices in here for alcohol that create a similar scenario with which to identify. Food, watching too much Netflix, online shopping, gambling, smoking, of course any other drug. You can also fall into a similar pattern with sex or pornography. All of these activities we think of as being enjoyable, and in the right doses can even be beneficial. Food can be a potent reward for good behavior, sex can increase our level of intimacy with a partner. Yet, it is clear that all of these behaviors can fall into patterns of abuse and become destructive when the behavior becomes excessive. (Don't make me explain to you why drugs are bad!)

Clearly, in my case, I was taking an activity I enjoyed (drinking) and misusing it in such a way that it was affecting not only other activities of my life, but more importantly it was changing who I was as a person. I was to the point that I felt like a shell of my true self. Any one of the behaviors I've listed can become destructive when carried to excess. When we take something that gives us pleasure and start overusing it to the point that we sacrifice other things and people from our lives, it becomes detrimental. From the outside, it seems so obvious what my problem was, but then why did I, like so many others, get stuck? The answer is because of my pattern of use.

Although it was an inefficient coping mechanism for stress, it's one I knew, or thought I knew, how to navigate. The pattern of Friday happy hour, to Saturday brunch, and Sunday Funday provided stability in my life, however shaky, such that regardless of whatever else was going on my world that week, I took comfort in knowing that there was some constancy to my being. I believe we all perceive our habits or our routines, whether they are creative or actually destructive, to provide us solid footing amid the chaos of our lives. As a result, we return to these habits, week after week, to alleviate the anxiety and fear in an otherwise chaotic and unpredictable world.

Addiction is both powerful and insidious. We don't often realize a particular behavior is a problem until it we're already hooked. Sure, there are addictions that are easy to identify. For instance, the dopamine surges triggered by cocaine, sex, and gambling are well-documented. It's easy to see why these activities can quickly lead to addiction. But what separates a "recreational" user from someone who becomes an addict? The answer is, routine. Humans long for routine in one form or another to shield ourselves from the emotional discomfort in our world. There is so much that is outside our control that we take solace in our routines as a firm grounding from which to view the world. Often, these behaviors are benign: our car commute to work, our cup of coffee in the morning, a TV show or book before bed.

However, for some of us, these activities are not enough, and other, potentially destructive habits creep into our lives. For example, a glass of wine in the evening to unwind becomes two or more. The sugar rush you enjoy from a nightly scoop of ice cream devolves into a donut or two in the morning and a pastry with lunch. The cocaine you told yourself would "just be done at parties" degenerates into a weekly or, worse, daily occurrence. The sex with your partner that made you feel so good may trigger clandestine affairs or incline you toward viewing pornography.

The problem with all of these actions is that they can easily slip into becoming routine in your life. What was once something that was novel or occasional has infiltrated its way as something you can't seem to get through the day without. Hence, the power of addiction. Malevolently, the real power of addiction is that it makes us believe we are victims when in fact we created the problem. You merely have to identify the maladaptive behaviors in your life and in doing so you can begin to unravel their power.

> *It is not in the stars to hold our destiny*
> *but in ourselves.*
> —William Shakespeare

Once again, it's time to take inventory and time to ask ourselves the tough questions. What is it in your life that has become at best a less-than-healthy habit and, at worst, a destructive one? Think about the rituals in your life—the things in your life that have made their way into your schedule that now seem impossible to give up. Is it the bowl of ice cream every night before bed? The all-day binge session of the latest Hulu series that seems to dominate your weekend? Perhaps you troll dating websites to pursue meaningless sexual encounters.

Or, maybe you are somewhat like myself and let a few drinks spiral out of control into an all-weekend bender? As we have seen, addictions can range from extremely serious such as stealing money from family to finance a methamphetamine habit to seemingly more innocent—such as neglecting our health or other relationships by spending too much time on the couch.

Whatever the case may be, if you realize that there is an activity that has, in some way, dominated or interfered with other aspects of your life, it may be affecting your family life, health, work, your spiritual or religious life. Maybe it's simply affected your financial affairs. Whatever the case, it is time to break the circuit of a destructive pattern and reclaim that part of your life. How to do that varies among us and depends on what exactly the destructive behavior is as well as how much a part of your life it has become. It can be as simple as behavior modification—for instance, not keeping ice cream or alcohol in the house, canceling your television subscriptions, or scheduling other activities during the time that had been occupied by the destructive behavior.

However, for more serious addictions, help may need to come from a professional counselor or support group; the problem may require strategies that are beyond the scope of this book. Regardless, the first step is to identify what has become a pattern in your life that no longer seems to be working for you. Recently, have you had any wake-up calls such as those I discussed in chapter 1? If so, take a deep look inside and examine what habits need to go. And as I mentioned in the preceding chapter, you can then develop a non-negotiable plan aimed at modifying or eliminating any destructive habits in your life. With these tools, some courage, and maybe even some professional support, you have the ability to end the sabotage on your life.

# 7

# Anxiety

## When Fear Becomes Toxic

Fear is a natural response to perceived threats and is an emotion with which all humans, and many animals, can relate. As a species, we are "hardwired" to value self-preservation through many years of evolution. A healthy amount of fear has kept us safe through the generations. Our ancestors who were able to stay safe and survive were also able to pass on their genes thereby instilling healthy doses of fear into the fabric of our DNA. Yet this did not come without a cost. Fear is processed in a more primitive part of our brains called the *amygdala.*

Although fear may have kept us safe from being eaten by lions or hyenas in the African Savannah, what happens to this neural circuitry when most of the imminent life threats faced by our ancestors are no longer present? I'm referring to the threat of being eaten by another animal, meeting a warring tribe of Neanderthals, dying from incurable diseases, and so on. Fortunately, modern man has all but vanquished such problems (although I swear I've seen a few Neanderthals still lurking about). It appears that the very same amygdala that has been critical to our survival does not like having nothing to do, so we find new things to fear, and when that goes too far, we develop anxiety.

Anxiety is a persistent worry or fear about everyday situations, regardless of whether they are real or imagined. Symptoms of anxiety commonly include palpitations or a fast heart rate, racing thoughts, sweating, feeling dizzy, a sense of impending doom, sleep disturbance, and irritability, among others. Anxiety can be generalized—worry about many different fears or about "the future" in general; or it may be situational—fear of speaking in public, to use a common example. Whatever the case, the fear is disproportionate to the actual threat. This is where anxiety differs from fear. For example, I am afraid to swim with great white sharks, but this would not constitute an anxiety disorder because the fear is rational and proportional. Sharks can, and probably will, eat me if they're hungry and I happen to be swimming in the part of the ocean where they live. Now, if I were to be afraid to swim in *any* body of water for fear of sharks, even in waters where there is no chance of encountering a shark, this would constitute situational anxiety.

We can all probably think of times we have been anxious or situations that have made us anxious. Going on a first date, speaking in public, or preparing for an examination are all situations in which anxiety is common. As long as we can manage the fear, and overcome it, then the anxiety, uncomfortable as it may be, is not necessarily a problem. However, in accordance with the *Diagnostic and Statistical Manual V,* more commonly referred to as the *DSM-V,* the reference manual used by psychiatrists, psychologists, social workers, and thera-pists to classify and diagnose mental illness, anxiety only becomes a disorder when it starts to interfere or impair our daily functioning. Thus, by definition, anxiety be-comes a *disorder* when it prevents us from living our lives to the fullest.

To summarize, anxiety is fear about what *might* hap-pen in our daily lives or in certain situations. We can prob-ably relate to inner dialogues we've had with ourselves in

44

situations such as "I'm anxious about my first date be-. cause what if she thinks I'm boring or doesn't like me?" or "I'm anxious about talking to my boss for a raise because what if she is critical of my work or performance?" These are common anxieties, and most of us likely have experienced them before. However, this anxiety becomes a disorder when it prevents one from accomplishing tasks.

In fact, when this fear prevents us from acting, the fear becomes pathological. I think we can all agree that someone who ends up being alone because of their anxiety about dating, or one who fails to advance their career because they are too afraid to explore career opportunities, is not thriving. They are essentially passing the reigns over to anxiety rather than being in the driver's seat themselves.

Of course, from time to time, some anxiety can cause us emotional discomfort. The key to overcoming it is to first recognize it, and then learn to manage it. As a personal example, I will admit that I suffer at times from anxiety before I am about to start a string of shifts in the emergency room. Emergency medicine is staffed based on a "shift work" model, and consequently, my schedule usually has me working four to six shifts in a row, and then I will be off for anywhere from three to seven shifts. I find my anxiety before going back to work is at its apex when I am about to start a string of shifts, after having been off for more than three or four days in a row.

Unsurprisingly, the nature of emergency medicine lends itself to fomenting this anxiety. The job is such that you have to be literally ready for anything that comes through your doors. You have no idea if you are going to see twenty patients in a night or fifty. You don't know beforehand what complaints you will hear, even if you think you must have heard them all before. (I once had a woman come to the emergency room *twice* to talk to me about an insect infestation she had at home. Strange as it may sound, she apparently thought it was my job to fix that.) I never know whether I am going to see a bunch of runny noses and stomach viruses, or a slew of heart attacks, strokes, and cardiac arrests.

Thus it's not always a far leap to let anxiety take over my mind as I ruminate about the possibilities that I might confront on my next shift.

For some, the fear can begin really to set in to the point that it has you doubting your own abilities. I know that my mind will sometimes start to wonder about all the "what ifs." "What if I forget the best drug to treat this condition?", "What if someone comes in with a problem and I have no immediate idea how to approach or treat?" or "What if the ER is extremely busy and in my haste to see everyone, I make a pivotal life-or-death mistake?" I am using my profession as an example, but truly any job has its own stressors and as a result its own set of anxieties. Fortunately, I am happy to say that despite this occasional anxiety, I have never missed a shift or let my anxiety interfere with my duties and obligations as a physician. This is not because I haven't been tempted to avoid the problem, or call out sick, but rather because I have identified my anxiety for what it is—irrational fear. In simply knowing this about myself, I have diminished anxiety's power to dominate my life.

Therefore, the first step in fixing any problem is to identify that there is a problem. So, think about your own life. Are there any times in your day that trigger the characteristic symptoms of anxiety? Again, there are likely many possibilities, but common triggers include anxiety about flying, driving, speaking in public, going to work, speaking on the phone, being intimate with a partner (Google "performance anxiety"), and many more. Are there any situations that you have noticed that cause your heart to race or instill a sense of dread? Are there times when you have wished you could escape, call in sick at work, or in some other way avoid doing a particular activity? If the answer to these questions is no, then you are fortunate enough to not have problems with anxiety, so feel free to skip ahead.

But, for most of us, there is at least one thing or some situation that instills a degree of anxiety within us. After we have identified these triggers, we need to come up with ways to help manage our symptoms and mitigate our fears so that anxiety does not prevent us from living our lives and achieving success.

There are many strategies for coping with anxiety, but I will outline what I believe have been the most helpful, nonpharmacological treatments, starting with something as simple as sleep.

Sleep is vital to our mental and physical health, yet it is one of the last things we seem to prioritize in today's age. Instead, the modern world seems to value those who can do it all, seemingly without sleeping. I am referring to the idolization of the person who can wake up early to get the kids ready for school, then work a full day in the office, only to rush home and shuttle the kids around to sports practice, playdates, or music/dance lessons. Then, they find time to get dinner ready, make a few work-related calls or e-mails, and eventually manage to get everyone to bed including themself.

Parents are easy to pick on because they have not only themselves to be responsible for, but also one child, perhaps more. However, even those without children to care for can succumb to neglecting the importance of sleep. The busy student with a full class load, a part-time job, and a penchant for late-night partying will often neglect sleep. This can also apply to the new lawyer trying to make partner in the firm or the new corporate intern trying to get noticed in the company. Regardless of the situation, the effect is the same. Lack of sleep takes a physical and mental toll on our well-being.

The physical toll is easy to recognize. We nod off in meetings, crave caffeine or sugar, or quite simply feel exhausted without the energy to carry on. Our physical bodies make us quite aware of the fact that we need sleep. However, recognizing the emotional or psychological cues for sleep is much more difficult. Common cues are irritability, inability to pay attention or being easily distracted from tasks (reading, listening), and of course, depression and anxiety. Aside from allowing our physical bodies (muscles, heart, and bones) to rest, sleep serves a vital function for our mental and psychological well-being. It is believed that sleep almost acts like a "clean-up crew" for our brains. Sleep is a time when neurons (brain cells) are nourished, synaptic connections (the way neurons talk to one another) are strengthened, toxic waste products are removed, and important neuronal chemicals are regenerated. With this in mind, it is easy to see why sleep is absolutely imperative to our mental health.

I also mention sleep first in the task of tackling anxiety because it is such an easy place to start both in terms of identifying the problem as well as solving it because sleep can easily be objectively measured. Simply think about your last week and recall the time you went to bed and then the time you woke up. Now is that time close to the recommended eight hours classically cited as the ideal amount of sleep for the average person, or is it more like five or six hours or less?

If you are someone who suffers from anxiety, and you are not getting close to eight hours of sleep, this is a great place to start on your road to regaining your mental health. Given the vital role sleep plays in our cognitive functioning, it is extremely difficult to combat *any* mental illness without first getting proper sleep. Think about how you are when you are tired. You simply do not have the "mental bandwidth" to process your emotions or handle daily stressors.

Lack of sleep often gives rise to anxiety because when we are fatigued our brains do not have the mental clarity necessary to prevent the more primitive parts of our brain from defaulting into fear when faced with perceived threats. Simply put, our cerebral cortex, where our higher-ordered thinking occurs, is too tired to control or override our amygdala, which you'll recall is the portion of the brain that controls responses to fear. Consequently, the solution is simply to make sleep a priority, or better yet a "non-negotiable," as I like to say. Sure, you might think, it would be nice to sleep more, but I don't have time. True, we lead busy lives with many responsibilities, which is why we need to reframe how we think about sleep.

For many people, sleep is considered optional, even a luxury. Yet, in light of the importance of sleep, is this really how we should think about it? What if we made sleep a priority and planned for seven to eight hours of sleep and structured the rest of our day around it? Instead of being the last thing we fit into our schedules, what about making it the first? You may say you don't have time for sleep, but is that truly the case?

Think about your schedule. What can you rearrange to make room for such a vital activity as sleep? You make time for other necessary functions such as eating and bathing, why should sleep be any different? Perhaps cutting back on television in the evening is a good place to start. Create more time by meal-prepping several meals for the week ahead of time rather than creating new ones from scratch each night. See if you can set up a carpool with other parents to taxi your kids around from their various activities and free up time for yourself. Be protective of your time at work, eliminate unnecessary meetings, work through lunch if you need to, and don't take on extra assignments if they will compromise your sleep. It may take some creative thinking to determine how you can make sleep a priority in your life.

After you have prioritized sleep, the next issue that may arise is falling asleep or staying asleep. Especially if you are dealing with anxiety, racing thoughts and worries can often prevent the onset of sleep, or may cause frequent wakening with difficulty returning to sleep. To help combat this, let's introduce the concept of sleep hygiene. Sleep hygiene is structuring and scheduling your sleep as well as the activities you do leading up to sleep in order to maximize the quality of your rest. The most effective tactic, albeit not always possible, is to try to sleep and rise at the same times every day. There can be some flexibility here, give or take an hour, but you definitely want to avoid wild swings in your sleep schedule.

Personally, as a night shift worker, I know that for some people this will be difficult to impossible, but for most people it is feasible. The next step is to create an environment conducive to sleep. This involves making sure your bedroom is cool, dark, and quiet, except perhaps for some "white noise," produced by the gentle blowing of a fan or soundtracks of babbling brooks. You want to avoid any harsh lights in the thirty minutes to an hour leading up to sleep. So, avoid all television, computer, or phone screens, and consider investing in low-wattage lamps with softer yellow lighting to be used before bed.

If you are someone who likes to fall asleep with the television on, like myself, most televisions have darker settings for their screen to remove any harsh lights (usually labeled as a "theater" or "movie" setting). Avoid eating anything heavy at least two hours before bedtime. Also, avoid drinking caffeine at least eight hours before bedtime.

Moving on from improving your sleep, there are also some activities that can help you drift off to sleep. Meditation, prayer, or breathing exercises for a few minutes can help relax the mind and signal to the brain and the body that you are preparing for rest. A small cup of a warm and soothing liquid, such as decaffeinated herbal tea, can also be helpful. Investing in dark "blackout" curtains or even a slumber mask (I found an inexpensive one online that works great, even if it does resemble a training bra) can be a game changer, particularly for you city dwellers who are plagued with excessive ambient lighting.

Speaking of investing in your sleep experience, this might be a good time to upgrade your mattress, as well as your sheets, pillows, and comforters. I will attest that finding the right mattress for your body is worth every ounce of time and money, as is upgrading to a quality sheet set. Fortunately, the Internet has made it more affordable than ever to find quality bedding without breaking the bank. Even if an item may seem too expensive for you right now, think about it compared to other high-ticket items we have no problem laying money down for such as cars, fancy clothes, or dinners out. You're going to spend seven to eight hours of your day sleeping, so it is worth spending a little extra on bedding to promote proper sleep.

Next, here's a tip for those of you who are like me and often have trouble falling asleep due to thoughts about the day's events racing through your mind or you're contemplating things you need to do the next day, tomorrow's to-do list. I have found it helpful to schedule some journaling time before bed. Keep a notepad by your bed for this purpose. You can also jot down notes about anything that may be bothering you.

The act of transferring our thoughts to paper can be very cathartic, helping us process our feelings. It can liberate your mind from needless worry about tomorrow's activities.

As for a simple relaxation technique for when those racing thoughts arrive, there is a breathing technique called "box breathing." This is very easy to learn and simply involves breathing in four phases, hence the term "boxed." First you inhale slowly over three seconds, then hold your breath for three seconds, exhale for three seconds, and hold your breath for three seconds before beginning the inhalation phase again. You can adapt this by shortening it to two seconds at a time or increasing to four seconds, depending on your ability (I don't want you to become lightheaded, or feel as though you are asphyxiating).

The next time your thoughts are racing and causing insomnia, try this for ten breaths or more. By concentrating on your breathing, you will be more inclined to forget about your stresses and be better able to relax into sleep. The last thing to mention, of course, is that if you sleep with a partner it is essential to make sure that they are on board with your changes in sleeping.

*You have power over your mind—not outside events. Realize this, and you will find strength.*
—Marcus Aurelius

Ideally, you should try to coordinate so as to be on the same sleep cycle, or if that is not possible, at the very least have your partner do their best to not disturb you during your sleep schedule. In short, these suggestions are certainly a start, but sleep is a complex activity and many books have been written about optimizing sleep if you would like to learn more. The goal here is to first have you understand and admit the importance of sleep, and second to give you some strategies to start improving your sleep. Doing so will certainly have a profound effect on your quality of life, but we are not finished yet. There are several other steps to be taken in our battle to control anxiety.

Exercise cannot be overemphasized as to its importance to our well-being. Sure, we all know that lack of exercise affects us physically. We are likely to gain weight and we lose physical strength. Lack of exercise is even associated with conditions such as high blood pressure, diabetes, and heart disease. However, exercise is also critically important to our mental well-being. We evolved from very active creatures: hunting and gathering in the African wilderness for our very survival. Accordingly, our genes are hardwired to crave and even require physical stress and challenges.

The sedentary lifestyle that has plagued the roughly last one hundred years of human existence is unnatural for us, and our genes have not had time to adapt. Ultimately, we require movement to be both physically and mentally healthy. Thus there is a profound wisdom to the classic expression "Go take a hike!" Similar to journaling or sleeping, whenever we are mentally stressed, physical activity allows our brains to subconsciously sort out our problems while we actively focus on a physical task.

While running, for instance, our brains are actively engaged in the task at hand, which involves coordinating the movement of our arms and legs, breathing, all the while not tripping over a bump in the road or falling off the treadmill. While this is happening, whatever problem was stressing us takes a back seat, allowing our brains to subconsciously process our feelings as well as potential solutions. As a bonus, exercise also releases natural "feel good" hormones called *endorphins* that elevate our mood all without negative side effects of pharmaceuticals. Similarly, exercise makes us feel better by promoting a healthy weight, increasing strength and endurance, and satisfying that ingrained genetic need to physically push ourselves. With all these benefits, it is a wonder why forgoing exercise would ever be an option. As I like to say, in what might become my new catchphrase, "Make exercise non-negotiable!"

Along with physical activity, we cannot neglect the importance of diet and nutrition. When feeling anxious, we often reach for anything that can comfort us, and for many that comes in the form of food, namely junk food. Similar to our need for exercise, our brains and bodies have adapted to crave rich, sugary foods, especially in times of stress. In centuries gone by, when we were hunters and gatherers, these foods were rare. However, nowadays, these foods are anything but rare and even easier to get than ever before. (Thanks to online delivery services, you don't even have to leave your home to get your sugar fix.) As a result, candies, cookies, cakes, ice cream, and the like are all too easy to reach for in times of stress and when we are in need of comfort.

Yet you likely realize that the comfort from these foods does not last long. After our glucose levels rise, and consequently our insulin spikes to bring it down, we are often left feeling worse off than before we ate junk food. Once again, we are craving confections to ameliorate the dismal feelings. Be aware of this phenomenon and break the cycle. Proper nutrition is imperative for physical and psychological health. Instead of high-sugar and nutrient-poor cookies, cakes, and pasta, reach for proteins, meats, vegetables, and complex carbohydrates. Complex carbohydrates such as whole grain bread, brown rice, and oatmeal will keep you satisfied longer and prevent the glucose and insulin highs and lows that cause us to gain weight. They also prevent the mood swings that accompany the sugar "roller coaster." I will talk more extensively about diet in a later chapter, but for now heed the old adage "You are what you eat." If you put less nutritious garbage into your diet, your body is affected negatively. Junk food, like many quick fixes, may seem helpful in the short term, but end up harming us in the long run.

Last but not least, let's not forget about the dangers of self-medicating, which is a euphemism for using alcohol or other drugs of abuse (cocaine, heroin, illicit prescription drugs) as a way to control your anxiety or other emotional problems. I will focus on alcohol here, but the advice here applies to other drugs as well. Medically, alcohol serves as a potent anxiolytic (a drug that reduces anxiety). In fact, pharmacologically, it acts on the same receptors as other popular anxiolytics with brand names such as Xanax, Valium, and Ativan. This receptor is called the *GABA receptor,* and there are many such receptors located in our brains. The GABA receptor is extremely important; it allows us to relax and sleep, and prevents us from hyperactive states such as seizures. Activating these receptors can be used medically to treat anxiety or panic, induce sleep, or treat seizures. (In the ER, I've learned that these drugs can be particularly helpful when a methamphetamine-fueled patient is trying to throw a chair at you.) When we take a drink, the alcohol quickly gets to work to activate our GABA receptors, causing us to feel very calm and relaxed. Many will quickly get sleepy. Any anxiety we are feeling soon dissipates, and we start to feel that we can do anything. Hence the term "liquid courage." Anyone who has drunk more than a drink or two in one evening can attest to this fact.

Take a few more drinks, however, and all of a sudden you may find you do things you wouldn't normally do. You finally have the confidence to talk to your unrequited love interest, start dancing, and, most importantly, sing karaoke. (I am told I am really good at singing after a few drinks.... I think....) Unfortunately, as is true in medicine, every drug has a side effect, and we can also do untoward things such as tell off our employers or even start a physical fight with someone—an action you would never take if sober. Moreover, alcohol, after its desired effects wear off, exacts a heavy price when we overindulge; several hours after we have imbibed, we develop a form of dysphoria (nausea, headache, dehydration, and even rebound anxiety or uneasiness). This is more commonly known as a hangover.

Lastly, although alcohol is certainly a sedative, and many use it to help them sleep, it is not a wise choice for insomnia as it disrupts the part of sleep we call the REM cycle. *REM* stands for *rapid eye movement* and is the deepest and most restorative phase of sleep. So yes, although that nightcap may have put you to bed, your sleep is often disturbed and not nearly as restful and natural as if you had you not had anything to drink. Given how important sleep is to our psychological health, it is no wonder that alcohol is a detrimental choice as a self-medication for anxiety.

As you can see, alcohol, like sugar and junk food, is a very poor solution for anxiety or panic. Even though it helps abate some negative feelings in the short term, it quickly leaves us feeling worse later. For this reason, alcohol is ripe for abuse. Similar to a sugar high, after the euphoria from alcohol wears off, it has many vulnerable people reaching back to the bottle to escape that severe dysphoria that comes from alcohol withdrawal. However, our bodies are designed for survival and we have evolved a brilliant mechanism to protect ourselves from death by alcohol for those who abuse it.

As you can imagine, because alcohol acts on GABA receptors to induce sleep, in suffcient quantities it can cause a sleep so deep (eventually to the point of being in a coma) that the user can be so sedated that they stop breathing. This is one of the ways that people die from alcohol. (Death can also occur because of trauma sustained while drinking.)

In order to prevent this, when our brains start detecting a steady flow of alcohol for days to weeks on end, they begin to remove GABA receptors from the brain (a process called receptor downregulation), which does two things: First, it decreases the chance that we will become overly sedated from alcohol; this is why a novice drinker may pass out after three or four beers in a night, while a seasoned drinker could easily consume eight to twelve beers in the same amount of time and still remain standing. Similarly, as time goes on, it takes more alcohol for us to feel the same euphoria we once had with lesser amounts. This condition is known as *tolerance.* Second, if a chronic drinker stops drinking abruptly, say for eight to twenty-four hours, they will start to experience extreme withdrawal. This is because the brain has downregulated the GABA receptors to the point that there are not enough receptors to prevent neuronal hyperactivity in the absence of alcohol. For this reason, chronic drinkers, in the absence of alcohol, will start to feel shaky, get palpitations, feel anxious, and start to sweat.

In severe cases, *delirium tremens* will set in; this involves altered mental status, hallucinations, and seizures. At this point, the person will die if not medically treated. Although alcohol is a tempting solution to anxiety, given its widespread availability and social acceptability, clearly it is a maladaptive strategy that can be deleterious at best and fatal at worst.

Alcohol abuse, and substance abuse in general, is an extremely complex issue, and this short chapter in no way does justice to the complexity of the issue. As I mentioned earlier, I once used alcohol as a means to self-medicate during my medical training. I wasn't on "skid row" by any means, and I was highly functioning—able to hold down a job and manage my other responsibilities. However, I realize now what a maladaptive behavior I was engaged in, and it has taken time for me to develop a healthier relationship with alcohol. I still drink today, but I do so in a much safer and less destructive way, thanks to having engaged in periods of abstinence, along with counseling. Everyone is different, of course, and some may be able to simply cut back on alcohol use, while others may find it's best to avoid alcohol completely.

This section of the chapter is merely meant to be a starting point for those who may be suffering from addiction by delineating the physiologic basis as to why alcohol is a commonly misused treatment for anxiety.

If you feel you have a problem with alcohol or drugs, I encourage you to seek longer-term help in the form of counseling or treatment at an addiction center.

In summary, anxiety is the result of the deregulation of our evolutionarily beneficial fear response; we may experience it generally, or it may be situational. By recognizing what triggers our anxiety, we can start the process of healing by optimizing our sleep, practicing relaxation techniques, and of course making sure we get plenty of exercise and nourish our bodies with proper nutrition. Lastly, we need to eliminate negative behaviors such as overeating, alcohol abuse, and other addictions. Dealing with anxiety can be overwhelming at first, but I hope that you feel better equipped to recognize your anxieties and begin to take control of your fears to prepare for a confident future.

# 8

# Don't Get Trapped

*Sometimes the Grass Really Is Greener*

On the way to our dreams, there are plenty of opportunities to get stuck. Any time we are going from point A to point B, there are likely to be obstacles in the way. That is to be expected. What I would like to talk about here, however, is something more insidious: settling. Settling refers to giving up. You stop pursuing your dream because you have become comfortable in your current situation. This situation arises when you realize things are not great (you understand that this isn't what you dreamed of), but they are just good enough to prevent you from being motivated to reach for more. This can happen to anyone, in any phase of their lives, but it is particularly prevalent for people in their twenties and thirties. If you don't happen to fall into that age bracket, fear not, this discussion is valid for any age group, except maybe newborns (but perhaps even they too can learn to reach for more).

I refer to this age group because this demographic is generally finished with their education and has begun working at entry-level jobs. This age group may have gone to school, received training, or simply entered their twenties with such hope for the future. They have a picture in their minds of what their lives will look like in ten to twenty years, but they don't seem destined to achieve that dream. They may end up in decent jobs with a comfortable life, but a quick self-examination causes them to realize that this certainly wasn't what they hoped for. Somewhere along the way, they got stuck. Now let's explore how it happened and what to do about it.

Before we begin, let's just clarify one thing. This chapter is not about being unhappy with where you are now. If you didn't make it all the way to the job or life that you fantasized about when you were younger, but you are generally very happy with your life as it is now, that is fantastic. Our goals and dreams can change as we age, and what we wanted for ourselves at ages eighteen through twenty-one (traveling the world or becoming a movie star) may be very different from what we want in our thirties and forties (hoping our kids get into a good school, or a new Swiffer, perhaps). Our priorities change as we age and so do our circumstances. Accordingly, our goals evolve as well.

This chapter is for those who have gotten sidetracked from where they thought they were going. I hope this chapter helps people recognize when they are going off the rails so they can make corrections before they wake up ten years later wondering where it all went wrong.

I had the "pleasure" of working in the food service industry from the time I was thirteen, all the way up until I became a resident physician at twenty-seven years old. I did everything from catering (I've worked so many bar mitzvahs that I feel I must at least qualify as at least an honorary Jew at this point), to finer dining, with pubs in between. I highly recommend that everyone work in this industry, particularly when you are young because you get to experience working with such a breadth of humanity, both in terms of your coworkers as well as your clientele. I actually think working in restaurants really prepared me for the emergency room, albeit the orders I take are a little different now. ("For our first-time patients I like to recommend a liter of normal saline to pair with morphine and a side of Benadryl.")

Of course, I could talk ad nauseam about the horrors of working in the food service industry, and in fact, blogs and movies have been produced about this topic. However, I have also met some truly wonderful people in this line of work, including customers with more than a fair share of interesting characters along the way. What would strike me most, however, would be those people who were exemplary at their jobs in the restaurant, but I could tell they were capable of so much more. I could see intelligence, ability, and potential pouring out from such individuals, yet they did not seem to be living life to the fullest. Rather than living up to their capability, they got trapped.

As an aside, please do not misunderstand me. This is not meant in any way to demean people who work in the food industry. I know firsthand that you can have a very satisfying and lucrative career waiting tables, bartending, and cooking. Furthermore, they are performing jobs our society needs and values. Virtually all of us go to restaurants or eat out from time to time; we appreciate the people who provide such dining services. Again, if they are happy with what they are doing, then congratulations to them! Moreover, this is not to paint the food industry as a dead-end either. For some people, working in the restaurant business is the career they are working for, and that is admirable.

However, I use the food industry as an example, not only because of my personal experience with it, but also because it is a field that has the potential to trap some people. When you are poor and just getting out from under your parents' roof in your late teens or early twenties, waiting tables can be appealing in the short run. You work in a fast-paced environment, usually with other young people, and get to work as much or as little as you would like. If you're lucky, your employer may provide you with meals during your work shift! There is often flexibility in your hours—you can swap shifts with people to accommodate your lifestyle. And, if you're waiting tables, you leave each shift with cash (from tips) in your pocket. You may remember thinking that you had never made this much money before or have had this type of freedom. If you want more money, just work some more shifts; if you want more free time, then work fewer shifts. As you can see, this can be particularly enticing, but after a few months or years of this lifestyle, one can easily lose sight of where they were headed. Before you know it, what was supposed to be a bridge until you finally got your resume together has now become your career. Perhaps you'd forgotten about higher education or getting your dream job altogether.

*Many of life's failures are people who did not realize how close they were to success when they gave up.*
—Thomas A. Edison

As an example, I'd like to talk about someone I knew, whom we will call Kevin to protect his privacy. Kevin was that all-American kid. He was a varsity athlete in college, went to a good private school, was smart and good-looking to boot. I met him working in an upscale restaurant and immediately forged a friendship with him. I could tell right away that he was bright, and he had an incredible work ethic that I admired. Rather than some servers who would prefer to complain about the work they had to do, or how little money they made that night, Kevin hustled and made sure he didn't have any "bad nights." Accordingly, he generally got assigned the best sections of the restaurant and made bank most nights. He was able to afford to live on his own, buy his own car, and satisfy himself materially. Sure, he had to work four or five nights a week, maybe with a lunch shift or two thrown in, but his fast-paced, cash-in-your-pocket restaurant job sure seemed to beat the humdrum of many nine-to-five jobs.

After a year or two of knowing him, I had entered into medical school. One night as our shift was winding down, we were talking about my time in school, and I had decided to ask him some questions about *his* future. I explained that I thought he was bright, college-educated, and still young and that he really had the world as his oyster. With his work ethic he probably would have been successful in a variety of fields. Furthermore, I continued to explain that his job in the restaurant *seems* great right now, but I challenged him to explore how he would feel in the same job, making the same money five or ten years from now.

In an effort to help nudge (okay, shove) him in the right direction, I even went as far as to help set him up with an interview at a national company that my brother worked for, knowing that he would thrive there. Yet, when the day came for the interview, he never showed up. (Yeah, my brother was *not* happy about that. Sorry, Matt!) The next few times I saw Kevin, he insinuated that he didn't want an office job. He said he didn't think he would be a good fit for an office job. A few years later, the last time I saw Kevin was in another restaurant, where he was working as a server. It was a different restaurant, different town, but same job, same Kevin. He was stuck. We chatted briefly and pleasantly, but we left it at that and said our goodbyes. I can only hope that he is happy, but I more so hope that because he had so much potential, he fully utilize that potential and either move up the ranks in the restaurant industry or move on to greener pastures.

As another example, there was an attractive, intelligent young woman, Stacy, with whom I worked at a pub. She was fresh out of college, and like many of us, she was wondering what to do next. Also like so many of us, she got a job at the pub as a "placeholder." She was amiable, energetic, and fun to be around. Working in restaurants, especially amid the din of a pub, seemed like the perfect environment for her. Of course, there was downtime, especially when we would have our "after-shift drinks" (I always found the best places to work), where we could talk about our futures. You could tell she did not want to be a waitress forever, but she did not have any idea what she really wanted to do.

She acknowledged the whole world of possibilities out there for her, yet having so many choices seemed to keep her stuck. For her, her current situation was safe. She knew the job, knew the menu, knew the customers, and this created for her a sense of self and security. There was little in the way of unknowns to strike fear in her heart; this strongly added to the sense of safety. For Stacy, leaving that job and trying something new was a frightening prospect. We humans crave order, consistency, and even routine; by having such order in her life, she avoided fear and anxiety. There is nothing wrong with order in one's life, and in fact it can be quite healthy. The problem with it, especially when we are young, is that if we are not exposing ourselves to fears and challenges, then we are not growing. That may be fine later on in her life but it is unlikely that she had achieved everything she ever wanted in life while only in her twenties.

Stacy was stuck. Unlike Kevin, however, who was stuck by the relative success he was experiencing, Stacy was stuck by her fear and insecurity. She would rather be permanently moored to the safety of the dock than venture out into uncharted waters. I haven't seen Stacy in a few years, but I did hear quite recently that she is still working at the same restaurant as a server or bartender. Again, all I can hope is that she is happy where she is, but part of me wonders if she is really living the life she wanted.

As these examples demonstrate, even at times in our lives when we are filled with potential, there is always the possibility of getting stuck. Those of you who are not servers or bartenders may think you are immune or that this chapter does not apply to you, yet the food industry is but one example of how we can derail from our future plans. Consider a young woman, an entry-level worker who may get a raise from time to time but never quite gets that "big promotion" to climb up the corporate ladder. The raises keep her complacent, and she can afford her modest lifestyle, but she certainly dreamed of becoming an executive one day. This could also just as easily apply to the small business owner whose business does okay but who is still slaving away to make the store run profitably when he had thought by this time his business would have franchised by now. Or, how about the more contemporary example of the blogger or Internet marketer who is doing fine with their work and able to make a living but never quite became the international sensation that they had envisioned when they had first started out. Whatever our profession or career path, there is the chance of getting stuck. The first step is to recognize it: have that wake-up call.

As with most things, this first step, introspection, is also the most difficult. It forces us to take a deep look inside, as well as try to take a look from the outside and really come to terms with where we are in life. We must ask ourselves if that is where we want to be. This is difficult because as humans we hate to admit we are wrong, and by acknowledging that we are not where we wanted to be, we have to do exactly that. There then may come a feeling of regret, remorse, or even anger, as we wonder where we got off track. Whether it was not taking that new job or promotion, not moving to a new city, not going back to school, or not leaving a failed relationship, the theme is the same. There will be remorse and sorrow over opportunities that we let pass us by, probably because we were comfortable where we were at the time they arose.

This can become a vicious cycle, but only if you let it. Here's how the cycle works: your present self realizes that you are not where you wanted to be because you missed an opportunity a few years back. You realize today that you can now resolve to change your trajectory, if you choose. Sure, you might not have an opportunity right this very second, but you could make a change if you resolved to. You could apply for a new job, train for a new skill, go back to school, move to a new area, or find a new relationship. However, this all sounds like a lot of work, so instead you convince yourself that you are happy and decide to maintain the status quo, just like you did a few years prior.

The cycle repeats, until a few more years down the line when you receive your next epiphany, and you wonder how it all went wrong, again. So, break the cycle. You need not be a victim. You simply need to admit where you got off track and work to get back on track. With the Internet, it is easier than ever to learn a new skill, finish a degree, or start a new business. Moreover, the Internet facilitates the search for new opportunities whether you are seeking a new job, considering relocating to a new city, or looking for a new love. There are even Internet-based lending platforms that can help you finance this next phase of your life.

Of course, you can still go the old-fashioned route and mail your resume out, make phone calls to new leads, or meet new people in person, but the point is, in today's world, there are fewer excuses than ever to hold back anyone wanting and willing to change their lives. This is not to say that this will be easy—in fact, this will be hardest. But as mentioned earlier, the first step is the hardest part: admitting you made a few decisions that did not serve you well and resolving to make a change. This is the perfect time to reread the chapters "Set Goals for Yourself" and "Don't Take No for an Answer." Utilize the strategies there to start getting your life back on course.

With all this said, I also wish to emphasize the importance of being realistic. Many will tell you to "always reach for the stars" or to "keep on dreaming"; however, just like the man who "wants to lose a hundred pounds by next month," if you reach for something wildly unattainable (such as going from secretary to CEO), you may never get off the ground. You might start off enthusiastically, with all the best intentions, but the minute you realize that, despite giving it 100 percent, you are not appreciably any closer to becoming CEO. You may once again decide that your life really isn't all *that* bad and then decide to give up. Just like the man who starves himself for a week only to lose one pound, you might decidedly give up out of a feeling of hopelessness. It's important to always keep your goals precise and attainable.

As I mentioned earlier, setting a goal to move from secretary to office manager is way more feasible than moving from secretary to becoming CEO. After you reach the manager position, you can reassess and maybe then you can climb to an even higher position, if you choose. The point is not necessarily to be the top dog, the point is to satisfy the very human desire to continue growing and improving. Nobody wants to feel like they've plateaued in life, and even fewer want to admit that it was because of a choice they made or failed to make. Start taking action toward developing the life you want, even if you start with baby steps rather than leaps and bounds.

In short, envisioning the life we wanted and comparing it to the life we have now is a source of perpetual dissonance to the human condition. For the younger audience, I encourage you to tread carefully as you make your way out into the world, constantly reminding yourself that although a job may *seem* good now, will it still have seemed like the right choice a few years from now? For those who might be a bit older, remember that it's never too late to better your life. Your age and experience are at your back to push you toward taking modest steps toward getting yourself back on track to your dreams. So, now, stop telling yourself you can't. Start pursuing the life you've always wanted.

# 9

# Managing Your Weight

*Get Off the Yo-yo!*

In today's American culture, weight is a complicated issue. On one hand, we hear warning bells from agencies such as the Center for Disease Control about the worsening "obesity epidemic" around the world, although on the other hand, there are self-appointed "social justice warriors" taking to the bully pulpit on social media sites to admonish "fat shaming" or to preach body positivity—the doctrine of loving yourself regardless of your size. Perhaps it is fitting that just like one's weight on the scale, our attitudes toward obesity can swing one way or the other. Furthermore, we are seeing seemingly schizophrenic trends in the market where even long-established fast-food chains, now fully aware of the obesity statistics, are offering more salads and arguably healthier options along with their standard fare.

At the same time however, these restaurants are increasing portion sizes, and it is now easier than ever via apps to have virtually any food you want delivered to your door, exacerbating our already sedentary lifestyles. With so many conflicting developments, the proper course of action for us as individuals is more difficult to discern than ever.

Let me begin by clarifying the goals of this chapter. This book is written with the goal of instilling skills and mindset to help increase your overall happiness, and this chapter is but one part of the equation for achieving happiness. The advice that follows is based on my opinions and experiences both as someone who struggled with excess weight earlier in life, as well as my role as a medical doctor. With that said, although I believe happiness for us as species has some generic requirements that apply to all of us, when it comes to weight loss there is no "one size fits all." We are all unique, and there is not one magic weight or BMI (body mass index) that is required for us to be happy. One person may love their lean physique or six-pack abs and be happy to put in the effort and discipline required to maintain that. However, others may be happier with some extra pounds; they find happiness in having a more liberal diet. My position is that both are acceptable, as long as you are healthy and able to perform the activities that you enjoy.

Life is about trade-offs, and you never get something for nothing. You may be okay with some extra weight around your midsection if it allows you the freedom to enjoy your beer, wings, pizza, and donuts. But physically and medically there is a price to pay. Physically, of course, there is a weight at which you probably simply won't feel good. Clothes won't fit right, you may have difficulty performing basic physical tasks (going up a flight of steps, walking more than a block or two, or even certain sexual activities), not to mention decreased energy or poor sleep quality.

Medically, the science is quite clear. Excess body fat opens us up to increased risk from a host of deleterious conditions ranging from high blood pressure and diabetes, to high cholesterol, all of which contribute to the risk of death or disability from more catastrophic ailments such as heart disease and stroke. Excess weight also stresses our skeletal system and can cause premature arthritis, especially in the knees and hips. The extra weight also contributes to chronic back pain as the extra fat changes our center of gravity pulling our backs out of alignment.

Even sleep can become less restful as weight increases, secondary to higher rates of obstructive sleep apnea, a potentially serious sleep disorder in which breathing repeatedly stops and starts. Conversely, it is well-known that even modest amounts of weight loss (ten to twenty pounds) can decrease our risk from the aforementioned maladies.

Consequently, I believe the well-documented medical science forces us to proceed with a high degree of caution against blindly condoning being overweight.

There are an increasing number of voices espousing the notion that size doesn't matter and that you should love yourself as you are and not be ashamed of your weight. Of course, I agree we should love ourselves, but when you love someone you take care of them. Knowing what we know about obesity and its risks, are you truly caring for yourself when you are exposing your body to an increased risk of chronic diseases? You are your body, and physical health is inextricably tied to mental health. I do agree with body positivity in that we shouldn't shame ourselves, and we especially shouldn't shame other people who are overweight. However, it is certainly a mistake to tell people that having pounds upon pounds of excess body fat is a good thing. Medically speaking, it is not.

Although being overweight doesn't mean you are definitely going to develop diabetes or heart disease, the risks of obesity are clear. Thus, what we should be doing is teaching people to love themselves, regardless of their size, and then how to care for what you love. Lastly, before we dive into the meat of this chapter, I will note that this section focuses on helping those who are overweight or obese. On the other end of the spectrum, there are the less common but just as dangerous conditions from being pathologically underweight; such disorders as anorexia nervosa or maladaptive eating behaviors such as bulimia nervosa are not healthy for us. These conditions will not be discussed in this book, not because they are not important, but rather because they are extremely complex problems outside the scope of this book. If you or someone you know is suffering from bulimia or anorexia, please seek professional help.

Okay, so with this disclaimer out of the way, if you have decided that you are not at your goal weight, and that you would be happier losing a few pounds, then please read on. Let's start with the basics. Modern humans physically resemble our hunter-gatherer ancestors, but our lifestyles could not be more different. Our ancestral kin were extremely active in order to survive—they had no other choice. Whether it was walking in fields and forests gathering plants and fruits or chasing prey, our ancestors had to be pretty fit in order to survive in prehistoric times. Even downtime was filled with physical play or standing/crouching. You had to carry anything you owned. The most available foods were high in protein, fat, and fiber, while simple sugars, honey, and fruits were luxuries. There was no pasta, deep-fat fryers, or donuts. Thus we evolved to subsist on that diet and lifestyle, and our genes still "think" we are on the plains of the African Savannah.

Compare that to today. The easiest and most convenient foods are high in carbohydrates, sugars, and fats (chips, donuts, muffns, and egg sandwiches). Humans today can go a whole day with virtually no physical activity. Perhaps we walk only a few steps in our homes or offices. You drive to work in your car and circle the lot for the parking spot closest to the door. (God forbid you had to walk a bit farther or take the stairs!) You get in the elevator to your office, sit at a desk all day, have your lunch delivered, then finally leave work only to get back in your car, stop for dinner at a drive-through on the way home, and end the evening by sitting on the couch to watch *Survivor* season 147. You fall asleep and repeat the process the next day.

Okay, so that's an extreme example, but it is not too far from reality. In today's age, many people have to make a conscious effort to make time for activity in their daily lives. With the advent of online shopping, for instance, you can even get clothes and meals delivered as well as groceries and pharmaceuticals without even having to take a step. The Internet has also brought us video streaming services that allow us to have virtually limitless entertainment without ever having to leave the couch. As a result, it is no wonder that we are becoming fatter and less fit than ever. Now, don't get me wrong, I am not suggesting we abolish these modern conveniences, and I admit that I even use many of them myself. However, we do need to be cognizant that although our lifestyles and diets have changed, our genes have not.

Our genes are still craving nutritious foods that can easily be avoided in the modern world. At the same time, it's easy to forgo getting exercise. So, if you are someone who has struggled with weight loss before, it is time you start working with your genes instead of against them.

Let's begin with physical activity. In centuries gone by, we, as a species, we were designed for long bouts of low-impact, cardiovascular activity. Most of the time, we were walking to gather fruits and nuts or to get from one settlement site to another. This was coupled with short bouts of more intense activity, such as sprinting to pursue prey or escape from predators. We had to lift heavy objects—our captured prey, stones, and branches for shelter. Climbing trees, walking up and down hills, and scrambling up rocks were all on the list of activities required. We likely did not do anything equivalent to running a modern-day marathon or spending an hour on the stair master. Rather, it was longer periods of slow to moderate intense activity, coupled with some feats of strength. Accordingly, centuries later, we need to adapt our modern lifestyles to fit this mold.

Previously, I discussed ways in which to work exercise into your daily life, so some of this may sounds familiar, but it bears repeating. As mentioned, fitting physical activity into your day can be virtually avoided given our modern conveniences. However, a little creativity can increase your activity and get your genes and metabolism working for you again. Is it possible to walk or ride a bike to work? What about walking to the train or metro station instead of driving? If you must drive, how about parking farther away from your office? Check your office for a stairwell that you could use instead of the elevators. Stairwells like this also make for a great way to break up a sedentary day. Are you able to adapt your desk to allow for more standing? Although they make desks now that can be adjusted to go from a sitting to a standing height, this could be done easily, albeit crudely, by simply finding a box or a crate to place on your desk to elevate your workspace. Use your lunch break to walk to get your food, or, if you brought your own food in, to take a few laps around the office building or street block.

Don't worry about how you look or what others think. This is about your health. All you need is a comfortable pair of shoes. You may even be surprised; some people may start joining you. Don't believe me? Just head to the local shopping mall (yes, those *still* exist) to find groups of people traveling in packs around the stores like their primitive ancestors roaming the Serengeti (though the cougars you see at the mall may be different from the ones our ancestors feared). You may just find your newfound zeal for fitness is contagious.

When you get home, make it a point to rely less on deliveries and fast-food orders, and actually go grocery shopping yourself. This way you get some more walking in and are more in control of what foods you are eating. After dinner, instead of plopping down on the couch, grab your partner and kids if you have them, and take a walk around the neighborhood. You will find this time spent being active to be much more abounding in quality as opposed to zoning out in front of the TV. Dogs can be great for this purpose as well. My dogs Willy and Winston are my not-so-secret weapon to making sure I get out and move every day. (They will let me know in not-so-subtle ways if I don't!) These are all simple ways to start giving your body the activity that it demands, but depending on your goals it can be just the beginning. The point is to avoid situations where you are sitting for more than an hour at a time, whether it be at home, in your car, or your office.

You will know that your body is thanking you as you notice improvements in your mood and well-being. You will start to find that by getting your heart pumping you'll increase your blood flow and will have a new tool to help battle stress. You may also find that your ability to problem-solve and tackle complex issues will increase. Physical activity allows your subconscious to sort through these problems, providing you the insight to develop innovative solutions or gain a new perspective on problems. It truly is incredible how uplifting even modest amounts of activity can be for your mind and body, all without even mentioning *diet*. But since I did mention the D-word, let's move on to that subject.

No doubt, there is a lot of good information available about diet and nutrition. However, there is plenty of misinformation. For example, we've been told for years by leaders in diet and nutrition the conventional wisdom that "eating fat makes you fat" and that breads, starches, and complex carbohydrates should comprise the bulk of our diets. They say red meats and butter are bad for us, and cereal and whole grain bread are good. It was simple and seemed to make sense. You are what you eat, as the old adage goes, so if you don't want to get fat, then don't eat fat. I can remember being in school and learning about the food pyramid, only to see it lived out in reality at the cafeteria. Lunch cafeteria lines were replete with pasta, pizza, sandwiches, juice boxes, and fruit snacks in an effort to adhere vehemently to the bottom layer of the pyramid.

Corporate America even followed the party line from the USDA, and they produced entire arrays of "fat-free" alternatives. (I'm getting nauseous even thinking about them.) Fat-free equated to guilt-free, so even if they tasted a little funky, at least you weren't being unhealthy, right? Before long, you could eat low-fat or fat-free cookies, cakes, TV dinners, pizza, and even ice cream with reckless abandon. Yet, despite having thought we had this all figured out, Americans, and later most of the Western world, got fatter. If fat was supposed to make you fat, then why this paradoxical weight gain with fat all but eliminated from our diets?

Figuratively, it is true that we are what we eat; however, the literal interpretation about fats is more complex than it was made out to be. It is true that fat can make you fat, but it turns out that carbohydrates can make you fatter. As a physician, I understand this now quite clearly. There are some out there who still subscribe to the notion that "a calorie is a calorie, no matter where it comes from," and you may have heard varying degrees of the mantra that "weight loss equals calories in minus calories out." These ideas, in combination with a misleading food pyramid, led to a generation of nutrition and exercise programs emphasizing strict calorie counting and endurance cardiovascular exercises. Because calories were limited, sometimes to borderline starvation levels, foods rich in carbohydrates were promoted as these food were less caloric than high-fat foods, and therefore, you could eat more of them. This was the age of the rice cake, and anyone who wasn't eating one must not have been serious about their health.

As we all know, in hindsight, these diets generally worked in the short run and almost always failed in the long run. The "yo-yo diet," also known as "weight cycling," is a term coined by the public health scholar Kelly D. Brownell, in reference to the cyclical loss and gain of weight, resembling the up-down motion of a yo-yo. If someone were determined enough to stick to the draconian measures proscribed in the diet, count their calories, run on their treadmill, and avoid fat, they would eventually lose weight. Many, however, could not get this far and never lost much, if any, weight.

If you did achieve your weight loss goals, however, it was only a matter of time before you remembered that fat tastes good, and you began to start consuming your usual favorites. It would start with sneaking in an extra snack or meal here and there; then people start realizing that treadmills are boring, so the exercise regimen also began to lag. Before long, the weight would start creeping back on, with many people finding themselves even heavier than *before* they started their diet. What is one to do? Well, find your nearest Weight Watchers or other weight loss center, dust off the low-fat cookbook, and get back on the now even more strained horse. It might not have been a long-term solution, but at least you looked good for your wedding, the holidays, or beach season. It seems unfathomable today how trapped many were, and still are, on the yo-yo, so now let's explore why.

It turns out that "fat makes you fat," and the idea that "a calorie is a calorie," is not quite the whole story. Yes, from an energy perspective, a calorie *is* just a calorie (nerd alert: in scientific terms, a calorie is the amount of energy required to raise the temperature of 1 gram of water by 1 degree Celsius). So if my goal were to heat a tank of water, the water would not care if I heated it by burning 100 calories of lard or 100 calories of bread. It would not know the difference at all, but the temperature would rise the same. (Note: This is the definition of a true calorie; when talking about food, as in what is listed on a nutrition label, we are actually talking about kilocalories, which is equal to 1,000 calories.) Thus, for the sake of this chapter, when we mention calories we are referring to kilocalories, as this is how the term is commonly used.

Of course, we humans are more complicated than tanks of water. Our bodies would react very differently to 100 calories if presented to our stomachs in the form of butter or pasta. The reason for this is due to the endocrine (hormone) responses elicited by different foods. Although there are a variety of hormones and enzymes involved in the body's processing of calories, the main player in this drama is insulin.

Now, for a quick, and hopefully painless, physiology lesson. Insulin is an incredibly important hormone, as any diabetic can tell you. The regulation of this hormone is pivotal to our maintenance of a healthy weight, as well as controlling our blood sugar. Insulin is released by the pancreas in response to increases in our blood sugar, such as occurs after a meal. The more sugars or carbohydrates that are rapidly absorbed from our gut into our bloodstream triggers ever larger increases in insulin.

Insulin is so important because it gives us energy by allowing our cells to utilize the sugars, or glucose, in our bloodstream. In other words, insulin is the signal that tells our cells to open the gates and let the sugar in. Once the sugar is inside the cell, it can be used for energy. This is all fine and dandy if we are eating exactly the amount of sugar (carbohydrates) that we need for the task at hand.

For instance, if we have a cup of orange juice, and then go for a twenty-minute run, we rapidly absorb the sugar from our gut into our bloodstream, and then insulin is released to direct it into our skeletal muscles to power our run. However, what if we have a glass of juice, a croissant, and a bear claw, and then instead of going for a run, we mosey into our cars and drive forty-five minutes into work to sit behind a desk. Insulin will of course be released; however, because it does not take us much energy to drive a car or sit at a desk, our cells will fill with glucose rather quickly.

The problem is that even though our muscle and nerve cells may not require any glucose at the moment, there is still a bunch of glucose floating around in the blood, looking for a place to go. Without trying to get too technical, the next place to store this excess glucose is in the form of glycogen—a form of glucose that serves as a means of energy storage. It is stored predominantly in the liver but also in the muscles. However, unless we are fairly active people, the chances are we likely already have enough glycogen stored from prior meals. Finally, with nowhere else to go, the glucose is directed by insulin into our fat cells. It is stored there as fat, which can be used later. Of course, if we are not active, the stored glucose remains as fat.

Now, I mentioned that a calorie is not *necessarily* a calorie, a calorie derived from sugar is treated very differently by our bodies from a calorie derived from fat; not all carbohydrates are the same either. True, all carbohydrates will be potent stimuli for our pancreases to release insulin; however, they don't all do so at the same rate. In general, the simpler the carbohydrate (table sugar, fructose, honey), the more quickly the sugar is absorbed and the more rapidly our insulin levels rise. As mentioned, this rapid rise in insulin is going to seek to shuttle the glucose in our bloodstream into our cells. If we are not actively exercising at the time, and our glycogen stores are already full, then the sugar is going to get quickly stored in fat tissues. If we have a more complex carbohydrate, such as brown rice or whole wheat bread, our guts take a longer time to break down those complex carbohydrates into absorbable sugars. This action slows their absorption and mitigates the rapid release of insulin. Instead of a quick spike in our glucose and a rapid "dose" of insulin, we get more of a steady absorption of sugar and a less-dramatic insulin response. This gives our bodies more time to use the glucose before it ends up being stored as fat.

On a practical level, most of us have experienced this physiologic response as the difference between eating a candy bar and eating some whole wheat toast. Both are high in carbohydrates, but the simple sugars in the candy bar give you a quick burst of energy, with a subsequent "crash," leaving you searching for your next sugar high. The complex carbohydrates of the whole wheat toast leave you feeling fuller longer without quite the same crash.

So, now that we understand that there are differences between carbohydrates, let's get the skinny on fats. Molecularly, fats are similar to carbohydrates, being composed of the same carbon, hydrogen, and oxygen atoms. However, the arrangement of the atoms is quite different, and so our bodies process them differently than carbohydrates. The key aspect of their processing to note here is that they do not cause nearly the same insulin response that carbohydrates do. Fat from our diet needs to be broken down into smaller molecules called "free fatty acids," which can then be processed further as an energy source.

Of course, fat can be stored as well, just like carbohydrates, but because of the reduced insulin response, fatty acids are not rapidly stored the way that carbohydrates are. Similar to the complex carbohydrate, these fats give our bodies more time to use the fat as an energy source, keep us satiated for longer periods of time, and prevent the crash many experience after a high carbohydrate meal. Thus, even though fat is more than twice as calorically dense as carbohydrates (containing nine calories per gram of fat compared to four calories in each gram of a carbohydrate), our bodies' response to fat may makes it more friendly to the waistline than previously thought.

For the sake of completeness, I should mention protein. Protein is really the good guy in the story, and not much bad can be said about the macronutrient from a weight management perspective. Protein provides four calories per gram of energy, just like carbohydrates; however, its metabolic impact is more similar to fats in that it does not cause a massive insulin release. And like fats, proteins need to be broken down into smaller units called amino acids before they can be properly used by the body. The amino acids provided by protein are important to our health; our bodies take the amino acids obtained from food and convert them into new proteins needed for everything from enzymes for our basic cellular processes to antibodies for our immune system. Amino acids also help build muscle mass.

Amino acids can be used as an energy source as well, but like fats, this requires some biochemical manipulation. Through a process called *gluconeogenesis*, amino acids can be converted directly into glucose. Consequently, because gluconeogenesis takes time, this results in a steadier energy source rather than the peaks and lows obtained from eating carbohydrates. Like fats, proteins give us the energy we need in a more even manner, keeping us fuller for longer without the crashes and cravings that often are the result of eating carbohydrates.

The last thing I would like to mention about these macronutrients (proteins, fats, and carbohydrates) is the idea of essentiality. When I talk about a nutrient being essential, I mean that it is a substance that must be obtained from our diets because we humans lack the biochemical machinery to manufacture these molecules on our own. Most people are familiar with this idea when it comes to vitamin and mineral deficiencies, which can certainly lead to disease. Fewer people, however, are aware of the essential nature of certain fats and amino acids (proteins). For instance, certain omega-3 fatty acids *must* be obtained from foods in the form of plant or fish oils. Our bodies require these fatty acids, and we cannot make them *de novo* ourselves from other precursors.

Similarly, there are nine essential amino acids that we must obtain from our diet. In case you can't guess where this is going, I am glad to point out that, interestingly enough, there is no essential carbohydrate. Amazingly, carbohydrates, which we have been told for decades to elevate as the backbone of our diets, offer no unique molecules or substances our bodies can't make ourselves. As mentioned, our cellular machinery can convert both proteins and fats into glucose to be used as an energy source. So, if we were to stop eating any carbohydrates altogether, our bodies would have no problem producing energy from a diet of fats and proteins. Finally, the cat's out of the bag when it comes to carbohydrates, so let's discuss what to do with this information.

As mentioned, the diet of our ancestors, whose genes we still possess, was quite different from our modern diet. Prehistoric man foraged for fresh fruit, mushrooms, and leaves, while obtaining the necessary proteins in our diets by hunting for wild game. Even the game they were hunting had a different diet than the farm-raised animals we eat today. Although fortunately the situation is changing thanks to more organic-farming methods, the case remains that many farm-raised animals today are still pumped with hormones, antibiotics, and fillers such as corn that, in turn, alters the nutritional content of their meat, which we then ingest. These meats may have different ratios of saturated to unsaturated fats and may be higher in pro-inflammatory molecules than the wild game enjoyed by our ancestors.

Books can and have been written about the perils of the food industry, so I will not delve further into the subject here, as that is not the point of this chapter. Nor is it my wish to completely demonize the food industry. Although there are downsides to so-called factory farming, we must remember that these farms

81

have allowed the planet to feed and sustain an otherwise unthinkable population of eight billion people. However, I do support as much as possible a return to a more natural, less-processed way of eating. So, in that sense, I do believe it is important to continue to foster the development of sustainable farming practices with fewer antibiotics, hormones, and processed feeds, while of course encouraging the ethical treatment of animals.

With that said, let's put this information to practical use. Think about your daily diet, or better yet, write down as much as you can recall about what you ate over the past three days Next, start categorizing your foods into high-carb/sugar and low-carb/sugar. Foods such as cereal, pasta, donuts, bread, sandwiches, ice cream, and candy would fall in the high-carb category. Salads (without croutons), green vegetables, meat dishes (not meat on a sandwich or in a burrito), nuts, yogurt (full-fat, no sugar added), eggs, bacon, and sausage would be considered low-carb foods. Don't forget to add any sodas, juices, or mocha-latte-frappuccino to the high-carb category. Now, take a look. Does your diet consist more of the low-carb or the high-carb foods? More importantly, are you eating some form of a high-carb food with every meal? This last question is of the utmost importance, as it seems to be a necessary part of the modern American diet, but increasingly of the global diet as well. Allow me to explain the main problem with this way of eating.

As mentioned, insulin is the critical hormone when it comes to fat storage in our bodies. So, consider the typical, modern breakfast of bacon, eggs, orange juice, toast, and maybe even pancakes. You have the bacon and eggs, which are high in fat and protein, which are not bad for us. You will slowly digest them, and there will not be a huge insulin surge in the process. However, once you add the carbohydrates in the form of toast, or worse yet, the pancakes swimming in maple syrup, you now have created a situation where your gut will quickly break down the carbohydrates into simple sugars, which are rapidly absorbed into the bloodstream, triggering a flood of insulin to manage the glucose load.

Once again, unless you are about to go for a long run after this meal, the carbohydrates in the meal will likely get stored as fat. The takeaway is that previously it was the prevailing wisdom that the eggs and the bacon were to blame for the rise in obesity and heart disease, but evidence suggests that it is actually the carbohydrates, with their resulting insulin surge, that is contributing to our expanding waistlines.

This makes sense. The molecular machinery of our bodies was not designed to handle a diet high in carbohydrates and simple sugars. In fact, such foods were a rarity. We've turned our ancestral diet on its head. Now it's time to get back to nature. I'm sure you have heard of low-carb diets before, initially popularized by the Atkins Diet, and the like. However, it is a change in mindset, and not simply a change in diet, that is required. You must start thinking about what you eat as a new way of life, and not merely "a diet" you will stick to until beach season is over. If you really want to take control of your weight, and more importantly your health, then you must "rewire" your brain to stop vilifying fats and start being careful about the amount of carbs you ingest.

So, what should you eat? Think back to what our primitive ancestors ate: nuts, berries, fish, wild meat, leaves, natural oils, and eggs. Conversely, think of what they *didn't* eat: bread, pasta, cereal, candy, donuts, juices, soda, and anything processed with chemical additives and synthetic fillers. Now, you might be thinking, I've heard this before, and it sounds good, but there is no way I can put this into practice. I once said the same thing. In fact, the first time I started to adopt this new way of eating, I had just moved to Astoria, Queens, in New York City, which is home to some of the best bakeries and bagel stores in America. Temptation was all around me, but I decided to give it a go and see what happened. Oddly enough, it was easier than I had thought to give up the convenience of carbohydrates.

The first few days were rough, simply because I had to break some long-standing habits. Sugar is addicting, so it certainly will take some willpower to eliminate it from one's diet. Furthermore, I was worried about losing the convenience of carbohydrate-rich foods. It was easy to roll out of bed, pour a bowl of cereal in the morning, stick a fiber bar in my bag, and head to work. A peanut butter and jelly sandwich made for the perfect portable lunch. (I was a poor resident at the time!) I rounded out my day with pizza, pasta, or Mexican food. Switching to low-carb certainly was not as convenient as a carb-rich diet, but with some ingenuity, the transition was not as time-consuming as I thought.

In the morning, I replaced my cereal with half an avocado, slices of tomato, and two or three scrambled eggs with cheese. I sometimes would make extra breakfast and pack half of it for lunch. That solved my lunch problem! I would keep a pack of mixed nuts in my bag at all times for emergency hunger pangs, but the surprising part was, I rarely needed them! In fact, the most amazing part of my new lifestyle was how profoundly my perception of hunger changed. Back when I was on a high-carb diet, I remember how, after eating a bowl of cereal in the mornings, with what appeared to be Swiss time clock precision, I would be famished three hours later. This was due to the rapid rise and fall of my blood sugar, secondary to the insulin response from the high carbohydrate load of the cereal.

So, once I ditched the carbs, I had found I could go easily five or six hours without eating, and when I did finally get hungry, I was nowhere near as ravenous as the sensation that plagued me after my morning cereal. I could easily make it to lunch, and then I would coast until dinner, which usually consisted of meat and a nonstarchy vegetable. Again, since I was a time and cash-strapped resident physician at that point in my life, I would buy whatever meat or veggies were on sale; I would prepare a bunch at one time to have as lunches and dinners throughout the week. Before long, this new "diet" did indeed become a way of life, and to this day, eight years later, I have no desire to go back to my high-grain, high-carb diet.

It is now easier than ever to ditch carbohydrates, and even restaurants and fast-food venues have caught onto the trend. With the rise in the diagnosis of "gluten sensitivities," the culinary world is catering more and more to low-carbohydrate diets. The secret to the success of the diet goes back to our physiology and how protein and fats take longer to digest. This keeps us fuller for longer periods. In turn we have a decrease in the rapid rises and falls in blood sugar levels; this prevents hunger pangs and slows down the storage of excess calories into fat.

*Always bear in mind that your own resolution to success is more important that any other one thing.*
—Abraham Lincoln

Yes, adopting this new way of eating will take some planning and involve breaking some bad habits. However, the results are more than worth it. Set yourself up for success by ridding your house of all "junk" foods such as high-carb, processed foods, cereals, cookies, and crackers. Replace these foods with nuts, fresh or frozen vegetables, eggs, bacon, canned tuna, as well as olive oil, butter, and mayonnaise.

If you are lactose tolerant, avoid low-fat dairy products and choose full-fat milk, yogurt, and cheeses. Pay attention to labels and avoid anything to which sugar is added. An example that is marketed as "healthy" (but is not) would be packaged yogurt with fruit added, which can pack up to a walloping forty or more grams of carbohydrates per serving, most of which is simple sugar!

By undergoing this purge and restocking of your pantry, you will not only eliminate the temptations that might derail your healthy eating habits; you will also rediscover the joy and flavor of many foods that were heretofore considered taboo (bacon, butter, and cheese). Hopefully you will learn to appreciate this low-carb lifestyle as an open door of new possibilities rather than simply closing the door on all the foods that were making you fat.

The last thing I would like to mention would be to emphasize the importance of lean muscle mass in keeping our weight in check. We already touched on the importance of movement and exercise, but I would like to add the benefits of some strength training. Increasing lean muscle mass in our bodies increases our basic metabolic rate, which allows us to burn more calories at rest, thereby preventing excess calories from being stored as fat. Furthermore, strength training prevents osteoporosis and promotes longevity. Now this doesn't mean you need to be a gym rat. Increasing muscle mass can be as simple as incorporating push-ups or pull-ups into your weekly routine. Also helpful for gaining muscle is doing squats, possibly while using household objects as weights. Or you may wish to invest in a set of dumbbells to make exercise easy. The point is not to get "ripped," but rather to challenge our bodies so that we can build and maintain muscle mass.

As an example, my fitness regimen consists of doing a set of ten pull-ups every other day, two sets of push-ups every five days. For one of these sets, I keep my hands on the floor with my feet on a sturdy chair. I also do sets of crunches once a week. Not that I am an Adonis (you can feel free to disagree), but I have been able to use this regimen to keep myself at roughly the same weight for eight years. Your routine may be different. If you are new to strength training start with simple exercises and gradually increase to work your way up. Keep pushing yourself to increase the number of repetitions you can do, or the number of sets, until you find a number you are happy with. The point is to firm up your muscles so they can start working for you in keeping your weight in check.

In summary, there is certainly a lot of information to digest about diet and exercise, so let's begin to put it all together. If you are someone who has struggled with weight loss in the past, myself included, this chapter gives you the keys you need to get yourself back in the driver's seat when it comes to your health. We first discussed the importance of activity and our bodies' need for movement. Later we also emphasized the beneficial effects of strength training and the role lean muscle plays in increasing our metabolism and keeping our weight in check. We dove into the different macronutrients and the misguided notions that carbohydrates should be the mainstay of our diets or that fat makes you fat. Using a brief understanding of physiology, we learned how adopting a low-carb diet along with increasing the amount of healthy, unprocessed fats and proteins can help us lose weight.

You have what it takes, right now, to make these positive changes in your life. In terms of where to begin, start by working more activity into your day and restrict your consumption of carbohydrates. How low should your carbohydrate count go? If you are trying to lose weight, I would suggest no more than thirty to forty grams of carbohydrates total in one day. Try that for at least two to four weeks and see how you do. Usually, within a month you should notice a significant change in your energy levels, hunger attacks, and of course, your weight. The beauty of this is that while you are counting carbs, counting calories becomes less important. No, that does not mean that you can eat as much of whatever you want so long as it is low-carb. It does mean eating "typical" portions such as three to four ounces of meat, a handful of nuts, plenty of nonstarchy vegetables, and one or two ounces of cheese.

This approach will likely cause you to be more easily satisfied, and you'll decrease cravings so that you can stick to the roughly 2,000 calories a day that most people need. Remember that calorie levels vary with age, weight, height, and activity level. Pregnancy and nursing may affect your nutrition needs; you may need to consult a specialist to determine your specific caloric needs. More often than not, however, after you minimize carbohydrates in your diet, you will likely find that you can simply listen to your body and let your hunger guide you as to the proper amount of calories you require each day.

Nowadays, weight is still a sticky subject, but maintaining your ideal weight is pivotal to your health, which is a huge factor in your happiness. Develop a "Don't take no for an answer" strategy to start a new way of life. And that is exactly what this is, a new way of life. In order to get off the yo-yo, you need to develop new habits that you can stick to for the rest of your life, not a short-term quick fix that leaves you worse off in the long run. Life is too short to never have bread, or pasta, or crème brûlée again, but it is also too short to suffer from conditions such as diabetes, hypertension, heart disease, and strokes. After you get your weight under control and your health back, you can indulge in the sweeter pleasures from time to time, provided an occasional indulgence doesn't become a daily decadence.

If you would like a more in-depth perspective on diet and exercise, I would recommend two books: *The Primal Blueprint* by Mark Sisson, and *Death by Food Pyramid* by Denise Minger. These books cover a lot of what we talked about, and much more. *The Primal Blueprint* delves even further into the healthy way to put into action a low-carb, high-fat, and protein diet. *Death by Food Pyramid* further delineates the problems of the high-carbohydrate, low-fat paradigm. Trust me, there is so much more to talk about, so I highly recommend these two books.

As a physician I would be remiss to neglect to add that you should consult your physician before starting any new diet or exercise regimen, particularly if you currently are dealing with medical illness or on any medications. Lastly, although I believe that this advice should help *most* people who are struggling with their weight, no two people are exactly the same, so specialized help may be needed in some cases. Furthermore, there is a strong psychological component to eating and weight, so please seek counseling or other professional help if you believe that mental health may be playing a factor in your weight-loss struggles. With that said, I empower you to get off the yo-yo and start reclaiming your health today!

# 10

# Financial Planning

*Money Matters*

A s the old saying goes, "Money can't buy happiness." I agree that this is true in terms of happiness defined as absolute joy or real satisfaction in one's life rather than mere pleasure. Certainly, however, lack of money or persistent financial stress can contribute to one's misery. Literature and Hollywood are replete with stories and examples of wealthy folks who have billions of dollars, servants, large houses, and fancy cars, but we may later learn that, despite all these material luxuries, they lead unfulfilled lives. The moral of the story is always the same; true happiness is about relationships and experiences, not about the size of your checkbook.

Not being a millionaire myself, I enjoy these stories just as much as the next person. However, it would be a mistake to demonize the pursuit of wealth or to make caricatures of those who have obtained it. This is in no way a chapter on how to "get rich quick." Rather I ask you to change your mindset about money and wealth so that money is seen not as *the* source of happiness. It is, however, a tool to obtain financial security, which is a pivotal foundation for happiness.

So money doesn't buy happiness, but it's clear that being broke doesn't buy it either. As the Western countries grow increasingly more into consumerist cultures, we are seeing more and more people living well beyond their means, while they struggle from paycheck to paycheck.

Increasingly, people are having to work two or more jobs to keep creditors and bill collectors at bay. This stress, running from job to job, takes a toll on our ability to care for ourselves and others. We forfeit sleep, time for exercise or recreation, and make poor nutrition choices as we careen from job A to job B. We don't have time to support or connect with spouses, children, family, or friends. Worse still, to make up for our lack of time and real connection with others, we fill the void with more material things (such as clothes, cars, gadgets, and jewelry) in an attempt to provide momentary pleasure to ourselves or loved ones, all the while plunging ourselves further into debt.

We think a new gaming system for our children will substitute for longer hours at the office, or a bauble or trinket for our spouse will make up for missed dinners or spending less time together. Clearly, money doesn't buy happiness, but stress over money certainly brings sorrow. In fact, financial stress is a top source of strain for couples and is a leading factor for divorce. Far too many people are working for their money rather than letting their money work for them and their relationships.

Debt is at the root of this problem. We are witnessing an increasingly permissive attitude toward debt. Virtually anyone can apply for and obtain a credit card, and most of us remember the mortgage bubble of 2008. Banks, government, and even producers of goods themselves are all pushing for us to buy things we can't afford with credit we likely can't pay back. I myself actually had to laugh when recently I went online to purchase some artisanal Easter candy for my partner and found out that there was an option to purchase these fancy chocolates on a payment plan! Even the confectionary industry is cashing in on the credit business.

Here's financial tip 1: if you can't afford to buy your candy outright, you shouldn't be buying it! It also left me in awe and trepidation to believe that there might be people out there who would actually buy chocolates they could not immediately afford. Although some chocoholics may disagree, in my view, chocolate is a quintessential luxury item that would in no way justify going into debt. Yet, nowadays, it appears that even chocolate can land you in the poor house. Unfortunately, this is the reality of our modern age. With one click of a button, you can buy something now and figure out how to pay for it later. Of course, the problem is that your future self will still have to provide for immediate needs a month or two from now, while being burdened with paying off things that were purchased in the past. Unless a decision is made to cut back, tighten the proverbial belt, and start paying down the debt, the situation will spiral further out of control. The predictable result will be the installation of more extreme austerity measures later, working longer hours, or bankruptcy—far from being a happy ending.

Credit, and credit cards in particular, are usually the source of financial woes. Used responsibly, credit cards can be a source for good, allowing you to safely and conveniently make purchases both online and in person, without the risks of having cash around. If you lose cash or it gets stolen, there is no getting it back. If you lose a credit card, you can cancel the card right away and even dispute and remove any fraudulent charges, mitigating potential disaster. Furthermore, if you pay your card's balance off every month, as I advocate you do, credit cards can open you up to a wide variety of perks such as cash back, travel miles, and even discounts at certain stores. Thus, used properly, credit is a godsend and can actually empower you financially.

Why, then, do so many people find themselves at the mercy of credit companies? The answer here is not the credit card itself, but rather credit card debt. For all their merit, credit cards have a "nasty" side. They are powerful tools to build debt. As mentioned, they are incredibly convenient, but a little thought experiment demonstrates the dangers of credit card debt.

Imagine you saw a jacket in a store that you really liked but didn't necessarily need. In fact, you are wearing a perfectly adequate jacket at the moment. Let's even sweeten it and say that the jacket happens to be on sale, helping you justify in your mind an unnecessary purchase. The total, with tax, comes to $87.49. It's not an overly grand expense, but you hesitate for a moment thinking that you don't really need the jacket, and perhaps there are other things for which you could use that money. Now, as you are preparing to pay, which scenario would make you less likely the purchase the jacket: having to sift through your purse or wallet to scrounge together and count out enough odd bills and change to pay the total amount or simply forking over a little plastic rectangle and paying for the jacket with a mere swipe of the wrist? Of course, it's the former. It is well known that when you pay cash, and actually have to hold in your hands the tangible money for which you worked so hard, you are way less likely the surrender that money so easily.

In one study by Prelec and Simester, people were found to spend 100 percent more (twice as much) when paying with credit cards rather than cash. I imagine this is because a credit card almost doesn't feel real the way actual money does. Besides, you won't have to deal with the fallout of any splurges or superfluous spending until a month from now. This system of instant gratification coupled with delayed consequences is how credit cards can create debt that can quickly get out of control.

Our little thought experiment has demonstrated the ease with which credit cards allow us to spend more than we otherwise would with cash, but worse still, when used improperly, force us to pay more for the very same items than had we purchased them with cash!

This is where the devil of credit card interest comes into play. Let's assume your card has an interest rate of 15 percent (which is pretty standard, although believe it or not most are higher). Now, let's say you decide you need to have a new big-screen TV for your living room that costs $1,000 total, including taxes and delivery. You don't happen to have the cash on hand, but you do have a fancy plastic card that will let you spend a $1,000 if you promise to pay it back. So you rationalize that you deserve something you can't afford right now and put the new TV on the credit card. You get the pleasure of enjoying your new purchase and impressing your friends when you invite them over for the big game night or the season premiere of *Love Is Blind.*

> *The best things in life are free. The second best things are very expensive.*
>
> —Coco Chanel

A month or so later, the credit card bill arrives and you now have to figure out how to pay for this large purchase. You still don't have $1,000 in your budget, but fortunately the credit company was kind enough to only ask you for a minimum monthly payment of $30. *Phew!* you think to yourself; you can definitely swing that. Thirty dollars is not too much to ask, and paying it off is not a huge imposition on your lifestyle. However, month after month, the credit company keeps asking for their $30, until finally, after forty-four months you finally have paid off your debt for the TV. *That wasn't so bad,* you think to yourself, forgetting that the TV would have cost you $1,000 had you been able to pay for it upfront with cash.

However, by paying only the minimum amount each month, all the while letting interest accrue, your "$1,000 TV" now has cost you $1,320, which is $320 more than the original retail price! You paid 32 percent more for something because you couldn't afford it.... Does that make any sense to you?! The credit card company thanks you for your support and looks forward to doing business with you in the future. Oh, and for a final kicker, the TV that you purchased now almost four years ago, is probably outdated, leaving you wondering if you should upgrade to the new model and just throw it on the card again. So, the cycle continues.

Again, this is not to demonize credit card companies. Furthermore, as I mentioned, there are ways to use credit cards to your advantage, but carrying a balance from month to month is not one of them. With that said, there are also times when we might be more justified in dipping into credit card debt, such as when you were laid off but still needed to buy groceries or had an unforeseen car repair you needed to make. I suggest you develop the financial discipline to be able to avoid using credit for these as well, but sometimes things happen in life despite our best attempts to prepare.

What you shouldn't do, however, is use credit to finance a lifestyle you can't afford. This is a quintessential distinguishing habit between those who are poor and those who are rich. In this light, credit card debt can almost be seen as a "poor tax." However, although many people are quick to blame the credit companies and so-called predatory lending, I hope that if I teach you anything in this book it is that you are not a mere victim and that knowledge can prevent you from falling into the same traps. You are in control of what you purchase, and you have the power to forgo purchases you cannot afford.

Interest on debts is a major roadblock to financial security, but there are other psychological factors at play that have become increasingly pervasive in our society. The most significant maladaptive behavior is termed the "hedonistic treadmill." Hedonism refers to the pursuit of pleasure, while the treadmill refers to the manner in which hedonism keeps us stuck in one place: usually poor and indebted. Another way to think about it is called "lifestyle creep," or even more colloquially, it's the perpetual need to "keep up with the Joneses." The hedonistic treadmill extends from the idea that as humans, we are far more loss-averse than we are to seek profit. As discussed in an earlier chapter, this means that, in general, we receive more displeasure from losing $10 than we would find pleasure in gaining $10. Consequently, this explains lifestyle creep, in which after we get used to a certain lifestyle, it is very difficult for us to tighten the belt and go back to a thriftier way of living. We simply crave more and more.

As an example, think of someone who gets a big promotion and goes from making $50,000 a year to $100,000. More often than not, they quickly adapt to the new wealth. They finance a fancier car with monthly payments that would have once seemed unfathomable. They upgrade from boxed wine to bottles (even bottles with corks instead of screwtops!). They buy nicer clothes and go to more expensive restaurants. This reaches a point where the extra $50k a year they are making is no longer able to finance these more lavish expenditures, so they fall back into the same habits of either going into credit card debt or living paycheck to paycheck.

Had they only modestly augmented their lifestyle, they could have enjoyed some of the finer things in life, while pocketing some of that money away for retirement or investment accounts. Instead, they stepped on the treadmill and continue to be a slave to purchases they cannot afford. Part of this is because most people, if not all people, enjoy fine wine, nice clothes, and gourmet food. However, part of this stems from the impulse to "keep up with the Joneses." We not only covet what others have, but we feel entitled to them as well. If my neighbor drives a Porsche, I should be able to drive one also. This envy or competition causes us to make poor purchasing decisions with disastrous consequences for our financial well-being.

The last, but related, concept that keeps people in poverty is the idea of being "house-poor" or "car-poor." This refers to the purchase of things that give the impression of wealth, while on the inside we are furtively struggling to stay afloat. Examples of this are legion, and one doesn't have to look too far to find them. This is the person who owns the mansion on the block, but has to work long hours to keep up with the mortgage and the taxes. This could be your friend who bought a new Tesla, but lives in a shabby apartment and never seems to have any money.

More commonly, these desires can take the form of simply buying new designer clothes every season and spending what you can on jewelry and cosmetics, while perpetually having little to nothing in your savings account. Whatever the purchase, the result is the same. You are spending beyond your means to give the appearance that you can "punch above your weight." Anyone, of any income class, can be affected by this. The dire outcome is that a vicious cycle is created. A purchase is made with credit for something you can't afford, you get used to this new level of luxury, and then you seek more credit for even more opulent items, creating not only more debt, but also an even higher status to maintain. Now that we have elucidated the many ways in which debt and financial hardship are engendered, let's examine how to break the cycle.

Let's define what I would consider the goal of this chapter: achieving financial freedom. Financial freedom is a state in which you are no longer controlled by worries about money. It puts you in a place that allows you to handle whatever life throws at you. So, what does it look like? Imagine you had no credit card debt and could pay off your balance every month. You spent only what you truly could afford, living within your means instead of above them.

Financial freedom means being able to be unemployed for anywhere from three to six months, let's say, and not having to worry about putting food on the table or paying your mortgage because you have either an emergency savings fund or other contingency plans (disability insurance or a home equity line of credit). It also means you are no longer living paycheck to paycheck, but rather are taking a portion of your income (say 10–20 percent) and investing or saving it every month for long-term goals such as buying a house, college funds, or saving for retirement. Imagine your car breaks down or your plumbing needs service, and you don't have to scramble to pay for it or put off the repairs altogether because you have an emergency fund.

In essence, financial freedom is peace of mind from the financial chaos life throws at us. We are finally able to start planning and saving for our futures, instead of trying to play catch-up with our pasts. Before moving on, I want to be clear that financial freedom does not require you to be out of all debt, but rather it does require you to eliminate bad debt such as credit card debt. Some debt is considered "good" debt if it truly is an investment in your future (mortgages, small business loans, and arguably student loans). Financial freedom does require, however, that you have a handle on even these debts and that you can make the monthly payments without a struggle. Now, having defined our goal, let's begin the journey of achieving it.

First and foremost, achieving financial freedom is getting control of your spending. In order to do that, you need to create a budget (even though budget planning may sound boring). I know this isn't glamorous, but I wouldn't ask you to carefully examine such planning if it weren't important. Your budget is like the heart of your financial plan: it directs where your money goes. If your budget is backed up with unnecessary expenses, it can no longer pump money forward to where it is needed (savings accounts, 401ks, and mortgages).

Fortunately, the task of doing this is very simple. First, get a rough amount of your yearly after-tax income. For salaried people this is easy; for those whose income is a little more variable, do the best you can to approximate, understanding that here it is better to underestimate rather than overestimate. Take that amount, and divide by twelve, this will give you your monthly income, telling you how much you have to spend each month. Next come the expenses, which will require a little thought. Start with your fixed expenses (the ones that generally don't change from month to month and that you must pay in order to be what most would consider a functioning human being).

Fixed expenses commonly include payments for things such as rent/mortgage, student loans, gas/electric bills, phone bills, car payments, fuel or transportation costs, insurance payments for your house, car, disability, and life insurance. Now STOP! Before we move on to variable expenses, I want you to add up all of your fixed expenses and subtract them from your income. Hopefully, you are still in the black (with a positive remainder). If you have found that your expenses already outweigh or come close to your monthly income, you need to make some serious cuts. Most often, this means you are driving a car you can't afford or living in a house or apartment that is above your means. The only other option to getting out of this situation is to make more money, which may be a possibility. But before moving on, pause here and see how you can either make a cut in expenses (downsize your house/get a roommate or downgrade your car) or upgrade your income (ask for a raise, work more hours, get another job) to get back on track.

Assuming your ledger is now back in the black, let's discuss your variable expenses. The money you have left (income minus fixed expenses) is the money you have left for everything else in your life, which constitutes your variable expenses. Food and drink, believe it or not, is a largely variable expense. Because it is mandatory to live, I could include it under the category of "fixed expenses," but I choose to list it here because what you spend on food can vary widely depending on your lifestyle. When it comes to groceries, are you a coupon-cutting, penny-pinching, bargain hunter, or are you a devil-may-care, "coupons are for grandmas," reckless shopper?

Furthermore, do you make your meals and coffee at home and take them to work, or are you eating out for virtually every meal? Same goes for clothing, which we need to survive, or at the very least be socially acceptable, but expenses can vary widely depending on whether we shop at Wal-mart or Chanel. Lastly, consider your other variable expenses such as entertainment, travel, pets, and gifts. Your variable expenses are in a way your most important (assuming you are living in a home and driving a car you can afford, see previous) because although they may not be the largest in your budget, they are the ones you have the most control over.

Not surprisingly, this is also the part of the budget in which people get into the most trouble. People end up having variable expenses that are so high that they end up not having anything left over for the most important category: savings. Without saving money every month, you cannot start planning or investing for the future. If you can't prepare for the future, you will never have financial freedom.

You will instead always be tethered to your job, working month to month to make ends meet. Thus, given the importance of managing our variable expenses, let's discuss how we can minimize them.

Wake up and smell the coffee! That's right, coffee is a classic example to illustrate how to manage your expenses. It's amazing how many people are sipping their potential savings right down to the poor house. Let me explain using two fictitious people as examples. First is Sarah Saverman. She buys a bulk canister of coffee beans for $15 a month to make her morning coffee. Because of the small expense, she is able to pay off the $15 every month rather than letting it accumulate as a balance on her credit card. On the other hand is Anthony Entitled. He works a fast-paced job and needs his morning joe five days a week. Rather than make it at home, he feels entitled to stop at his local Starbrokes, the fancy coffee shop near his office. He orders large coffee or sometimes even a cappuccino with an extra espresso, averaging $4 every morning after tax and tip (you really do have to tip everyone these days!). So, $4 a day times twenty work days a month equals $80 a month spent on coffee. Right off the bat, that's $65 a month over what Sarah pays that could go toward savings or investing (or paying down debt). To make matters worse, imagine that Anthony uses his credit card to pay for his morning coffee, but he only pays the minimum balance on the card. His $80 a month in coffee actually cost him $99 a month after interest, putting him now at $84 a month behind Sarah in achieving financial freedom! There are many people for whom $84 a month would go a long way in helping to pay off other expenses.

Okay, so maybe you don't drink coffee, but most of us have something similar to an expense like this in our lives. Maybe it's a morning bagel with cream cheese and a juice or ordering out for lunch every day. The point is that if you have not achieved financial freedom, these are the low-hanging fruit you should go after. It is much cheaper to make your coffee or your lunch at home and take it in. Moreover, to put things in perspective, if you are an entry-level employee making $10–$15 per hour, your morning coffee and ordered-out lunches can easily cost you an entire hour of your time...every day. Assuming you work eight hours a day, and twenty days a month, you just spent two and a half day's income so that you can order lunch and coffee out! Your money is your time. It is something to think about before that next latte.

Are you a smoker? A pack-a-day habit could easily be costing you between $200 and $300 a month. If you could cut back, or quit altogether, it would be the best thing you could do for your health and finances! I could go on and on, but I think you get the point. Expenses such as name-brand clothing, movie, athletic or concert tickets (with their overpriced concessions), and eating/drinking out can be expensive; the markup on alcohol in bars and restaurants in particular is absurd. These are all places you should be looking to cut if you have debt or do not meet the definition of financial freedom.

Now, this is not to say that we all must live like misers, and I am not advocating that at all. We all need to let our hair down every now and then, and treat ourselves to a night out or a nice dinner. My point is that there are so many purchases we make automatically, without thinking, that are deleterious to our financial well-being. Furthermore, there are so many simple ways that we can save that add up to real savings in the short and long run.

For example, do you buy a can of soda from the kiosk or vending machine for $1 a can, or do you plan ahead and buy a twelve-pack from the grocery store for $5? If you buy one can at a time, you are paying more than twice as much for the convenience. Are you spending $1 per bottle on water when in all likelihood water from the tap is just as good, or you could invest in a filter and take your own water from home? Again, it is by no means a mortal sin to buy a can of soda from a vending machine once in a while, but if this is a habit and you are struggling financially, then this is an easy place to start cutting costs.

So, start taking control of your spending. When buying clothes, look for sales (after holidays or end-of-season are particularly good times). Going out for food or drinks? Look for happy hours or see what daily specials they might be offering. Apps such as Groupon, Honey, and Rakuten can help make sure you never miss a coupon and may even help you get money back with purchases. For entertainment, depending on where you live, you'd be surprised at what you can do for little to no money. Of course, you could always take a walk around town or in a park, but often there are museums that have certain hours that do not require admission fees, theaters that offer discount tickets at off-peak times, or bars and restaurants may feature live music and all you need to do is buy a beer or a snack. Bottom line is that when striving for financial freedom, you need to be defensive of your money and not simply give it away merely for convenience alone. Now is the time to cinch the belt and figure out creative ways to be careful with your money so that you can focus on the ticket to freedom: savings.

"A penny saved is a penny earned" is well-known wisdom. However, depending on where you save your pennies, a penny saved can be much more than a penny earned. How is this possible? Through the miracle of investing and compound interest. The concept is probably familiar to most, but essentially compound interest is the process whereby an investment grows in an exponential fashion through reinvestment of money earned over time. In short, you are earning interest on interest. I actually already introduced this concept, albeit in a negative light when discussing the dangers of credit card debt. In that case, however, it was the lenders and credit card companies who were profiting from compound interest. (Anthony was paying the credit card companies $19 extra so that he could enjoy his daily coffee; the extra money is the result of compound interest on his debt.) Now, however, after you have your spending in check, it's time to get your money to start working for you.

The simplest, and most common, way to do this is to have a savings account. Most of us don't think about it this way, but savings accounts are investment accounts. You give the bank the permission to hold your money, and they promise to keep it safe. However, they are actually using your money to invest (usually in the form of loans to other customers), so in exchange for you letting them use your money, they offer you a rate of return. Because you are taking virtually no risk in this transaction, your rate of return is generally meager at best (a good interest rate these days is sadly around 1.5 percent). Even so, let's say that you are able to eliminate your debts and scrounge up $1,000 to put in a savings account with a 1.5 percent interest rate. Even if you just left that money in the bank and didn't take or add to it, in ten years you would have $1,161.73. In thirty years you would have $1,567.87! You made money without having to do anything except have the discipline to save it. Naturally, the situation is a little more complicated when you factor in taxes and inflation, but this simple example demonstrates that you can have your money working for you.

Of course, no one would suggest you are going to get rich by keeping your money in a savings account. Remember, you are accepting a measly rate of return in exchange for the safety and security a bank provides. Furthermore, the purpose of this chapter is not to teach you how to invest to become a millionaire (I suggest you look elsewhere for that; I've been told doctors make lousy investors!), it is to teach you how to achieve financial freedom to allow for a happier life. To illustrate further, and hopefully inspire you, we'll use the example from the prior paragraph but modify it only slightly. Again, let's say you had the same $1,000 you saved in a bank account at an interest rate of 1.5 percent, but this time, thanks to some mild frugality you are able to deposit an extra $100 into the account every month. If you do this automatically for thirty years, instead of having only $1,567.87, you would have a whopping $47,054.38 in your account! Sure, not enough to retire on, but nothing to sneeze at either. The point is that when you break down the numbers, you end up with roughly $47,000, even though the amount of money you ended up depositing into the account amounts to $37,000 over those thirty years. You made a profit of $10k, without having to do anything but save. As you can see, thanks to compound interest, savings over time can really add up.

Imagine how much money you would earn over time if you could save even more every month. As mentioned, however, a simple savings account is not the best place to keep your money from an investment standpoint. If you truly want to get on track for retirement, then you will need a little more bang for your buck. This is where an often overlooked account can be your ticket to financial freedom. It is the 401k. Of course, depending on your job you may or may not have access to a 401k (I will talk about what you can do in that case a little later), but because many people do and given its many benefits, I would be remiss not to advocate for this option. Again, books can and have been written about 401k plans and investing, so I am going to keep it simple here and hopefully demonstrate why you should try to invest as much as you can in your 401k if you have the option to do so.

First, the money you contribute is pre-tax. This means that your contributions come from your gross salary, which limits your tax liability. As an example, if you make $100,000 a year, but contribute $20,000 to your 401k, from the government's perspective when April 15th comes around, you would only be taxed as if you made $80,000, not $100,000. Similarly, the money in your 401k is allowed to grow tax-free as long as it's in the account. You will end up paying taxes on that money eventually when you retire, but you will likely be in a lower tax bracket when you finally start withdrawing money from your 401k. Secondly, the interest rate of return on a 401k is generally 5 to 8 percent, which is much better than the pitiful 1.5 percent you would earn in a savings account. So, if you had $1,000 in a 401k, and contributed $100 to it every month at a rate of 5 percent, after 30 years you would end up with close to $88,000 instead of the $47,000 you would have earned in a 1.5 percent savings account. If your 401k account did particularly well and earned 8 percent on average, you would earn almost $160,000, even with the same monthly contributions! Regardless, either way we are now talking about some serious numbers toward your retirement.

Lastly, the other reason you should take advantage of your 401k is if your employer offers any sort of match for your contributions. What this means is that your employer will match some percentage of your contributions up to a percentage of your salary (most commonly, employers will contribute fifty cents for every dollar you contribute, up to a maximum of 6 percent of your salary). So let's say you make $100,000, and you contribute $10,000 a year into your 401k, your employer will also donate $5,000 into your 401k account, free of charge. In reality, instead of making a salary of $100,000, you actually are making a salary of $105,000! It's free money, right there for the taking, yet oddly enough, many people pass by this. Either they are not aware of this benefit or they are living paycheck to paycheck already and can't imagine a smaller check in the shorter term, even if it means much more money in the long term.

If you are in the latter group, reread the earlier sections on this chapter to see if there are any ways you can minimize your expenses. If you fall into the former group, you can no longer plead ignorance, so I would discuss with your employer whether they offer a 401k with any matching. Then see how you can start getting your contributions on track.

Now, if you are not fortunate enough to have a 401k program, do not despair. There are plenty of other options for you. Most major banks offer investment products such as mutual funds, bond certificates, and Roth IRAs. While delving into the numerous investing options is outside of the scope of this book, the point still holds that you should be first saving money, and then investing that money at the best interest rate you can find, without exposing your money to unnecessary risks. I suggest pursuing accounts with interest rates of 5 to 8 percent. Any lower and you simply won't be achieving the returns necessary to power your retirement and any higher you might be incurring too much risk of losing your investments.

Yes, investment is a risk and there are no guarantees in life. You are paying for the safety and security of a bank account with a low interest rate, so in general the higher the rate of return on an investment the more likely it is that the investment could bust. We've all heard the tales of day traders who have gone from rags to riches and then rags again riding the waves of the markets. I certainly would not suggest that you should try to be one of those investors. Instead, do your own research either through books or on the Internet, or talk to a financial advisor if you need to determine what investment accounts are appropriate for you and your retirement goals.

Lastly in terms of investing, banks, stock market, and investment accounts aren't the only ways to have your money work for you. Buying real estate, becoming a landlord, and starting or investing in a small business are all other great ways to diversify yourself and build wealth. I encourage you to explore these options while being careful with your money: remember, if it seems too good to be true, it probably is.

In closing, I would like to add that I have been using an example of someone who has thirty years or so until retirement, do not despair if you might only have five, ten, or twenty years. Although less time is on your side, the principles are still the same. The major difference is that since you lack the advantage of time working for you in building compound interest, you need to rely more heavily on saving money to invest. This means instead of putting $100 away a month, you will need to put larger sums of money away. The other way to maximize your retirement fund would be to increase your rate of return, but I must caution you here to remember that higher returns usually mean higher risks, and if you don't have long until you want to retire, you probably cannot afford to be too risky either.

So, if you are in your fifties or sixties and hoping to retire someday, I encourage you to cut your expenses and start saving/investing, but depending on your financial health, you may need to adjust what retirement looks like to you. This may mean pushing back your retirement, working part-time in "retirement," or adjusting your lifestyle in retirement. Live more modestly. Perhaps you can move in with family. Regardless, although we cannot change choices or mistakes we've made in the past, it is never too late to start improving your future. So no, although you might not retire at sixty-five in a beach house on Maui, you certainly can take steps to make sure you are comfortable at an older age.

Speaking of retirement, that brings me to the last concept I would like to introduce in this chapter and that is financial independence. Although financial freedom is a state in which money is no longer a worry or concern due to your preparedness, financial independence means you no longer have to work for a living. Naturally, this is a prerequisite for retirement, but you don't have to wait until sixty-five for this to happen, nor do you have to be "in the top 1 percent" of wage earners to reach financial independence. Imagine how nice it would be to work because you want to and not because you have to, or to have more time to travel or spend with family and friends instead of being beholden to a job. Well, by minimizing your expenses, living within your means, and investing your money, this dream can become a reality.

By following the advice in this chapter and con-tinuing to educate yourself about finances, many people could achieve financial independence in their fifties or sooner. In order for you to live, however, someone needs to work, so the decisions you make now will determine whether it's you who has to do the work, or will it be your money?

I have touched on the importance of saving and investing, but I have barely scratched the surface on these important topics, so I encourage you to explore further, given how important financial health is to our physical and mental health. In essence, the chapter comes down to learning how to reduce your expenses so you can start saving money for investing. This is easier said than done, of course, so the next step is for you to take some time to start mapping out your expenses and seeing where cuts can be made. Start with your income and subtract your fixed expenses. If you haven't done so already, you should now create a new fixed expense called "savings." This can be in the form of money going to a 401k or other retirement account, or toward a savings account for a big purchase such as a house or emergency fund.

Just remember not to keep too much money in a simple savings account or you won't be benefiting as much from interest. How much should you be saving? Most sources will say the goal should be 20 percent of your income, but that is somewhat variable depending on your income, current financial health, and your age. If 20 percent seems impossible for you right now, then shoot for something lower, maybe even 5 or 10 percent, but at the very least start saving something. You can work up to 20 percent after your financial situation changes and you start developing good habits.

After you have subtracted your fixed expenses from your income, this is how much money you have left over for everything else—your variable expenses. What I personally do, and of course recommend, is that you download an app to help keep track of your variable spending. I myself use an app called Spending Tracker, but there are many others out there. I take the amount I have left over after fixed expenses (and savings) are accounted for, and enter that amount into an app. Every time I make a purchase (food, clothes, concert tickets, books, and okay, wine), I log it into the app as a deduction from my "spending money" for the month. This way, I keep track in real time of how much I have to spend. I know right away where I stand financially and no longer have to guess if I can afford to go out to a fancy dinner or spring for new clothes.

Of course you don't have to spend all the money you have leftover, but it is really helpful to know exactly where you stand. This does require some discipline, but the convenience of the app helps to allow it quickly to become a habit. Before long, you will gain control of your spending and make sure never again to go overboard and plummet back into unnecessary debt.

Again, I am not advocating for being a Scrooge, nor am I saying you can't splurge on a latte or a new coat. There is a certain joy that material things can bring us and arguably add to the richness of life. I am saying that you do need to make sure that these luxuries aren't robbing you of true happiness, and more importantly your future. I encourage you to live within your means by using the strategies mentioned in this chapter. Learn more by doing research into financial literacy. However you decide to do it, after you have control of your expenses, eliminate your debts, and have started saving, you will finally get into the driver's seat, and you will be on the road to financial freedom and, hopefully, independence.

# 11
# To Thine Own Self Be True
*Should You Care What Others Think?*

In many ways we are fortunate to live in an age where a premium is placed on self-expression. Through avenues such as Facebook, Twitter, YouTube, Instagram, and TikTok, there is no shortage of ways to show the world who you are. For better or worse, technology allows virtually anyone with a computer or smartphone to become a star in the reality show of their lives. With such liberation, it is a wonder then why substance abuse, anxiety, and depression are on the rise?

Although this is certainly a complex question, part of it stems from the simple fact that oftentimes we can place too high a premium on what others think. Regardless of the life and persona we display on social media, there is a strong desire for us to be accepted by others, with a consequent depression or sense of inadequacy should we fail to meet that goal, whether our failure is real or imagined.

I would like to preface the chapter with a caveat. To a degree, we *should* care about what others think. Yes, that's right, I am contradicting what has become an unassailable maxim in our modern culture. What I mean is that yes, you need to be true to yourself, and be real, or rather not be fake, but we live in a structured society, which means that you do need to find a way to fit in. In a nutshell, you need to be likable, at least in certain situations. For example, if you are a student or an entry-level employee or trainee, then being likable and approachable is integral to your success. The more congenial you are, the more likely people are going to want to be around you, and thus foster and nurture your education and development. Accordingly, I argue that it is not true that we can always just "be ourselves" and expect to get away with it. Living in a complex and increasingly interdependent society, we need to sometimes charm or cajole others into working with us.

If you think that you are going to make it to the top by saying whatever is on your mind or always putting yourself first, then you are likely going to find that people probably won't want much to do with you. Not to say you can never make it to the top with this approach, but if you are relying on people to take you under their wing, then it's best to demonstrate that you know your place and respect the value and place of others.

This is not an excuse or command to be fake to others. Rather, it is advice to remain cordial, especially when dealing with others where there is a power differential. Of course, I encourage you to be kind to others always, but I advise it especially so when you need someone to do something for you. This can be a teacher trying to teach you something, or a supervisor who needs to train you, or a barista making your coffee.

However, instead of being kind and biting your tongue, perhaps you would prefer to tell your teacher his breath stinks or his clothes are outdated, or tell your supervisor she's overpaid or incompetent, or the barista that he's too emo and that's not really a thing anymore. Whatever the case may be, the point is that being "true to yourself," saying what's on your mind or "keeping it real" may not always be the best strategy, nor is it in your best interest. You need your teacher to teach you, your supervisor to guide you, and your barista to get your coffee right without any unwanted ingredients. Presenting yourself in an affable way and learning to keep your mouth shut at the right times, will go a long way in availing yourself of new opportunities.

For example, while working at a restaurant I had the displeasure of training a woman whom I will call April. April was your quintessential know-it-all and completely lacked self-awareness. When she wasn't talking about how smart she was or telling you how "really creative" she was, she was likely botching an order from a table. We all make mistakes, of course; however, the difference was that when April made a mistake rather than listen and try to understand what she did wrong, she would try to explain what you were saying to her, back to you, as if she knew it the whole time.

This was quite irritating. Rather than express some humility, or listen and understand, she felt the need to always get a word in. Yeah...she didn't last very long. Maybe she was smart, and maybe she was creative, but sometimes in life, you have to accept your role and be willing to take instruction. Sometimes people actually do know something you don't, but you will never know unless you take time to listen.

Lastly, before getting to the heart of the chapter, I would just like to make it clear that I do not mean you should tolerate any form of discrimination based on the things you cannot change. If you have reason to believe that you are being targeted or discriminated against because of your race, gender, religion, or sexual orientation, then this is an instance where you do need to speak up, even if the perpetrator is superior to you in some way. If this is the case, American law is quite clear that this is inappropriate and illegal. I encourage you to take action in the appropriate channels such as human resources or school administrators. This is certainly not the time to bite your tongue or grin and bear it.

Okay, so now let's talk about when you should not care about what others think. We'll stick to some concepts rather than the infinite number of situations in which you shouldn't care about the opinions of others. The first is when it comes to being true to who you really are. This could be in regard to your religion, your sexuality, or just your preferences in general. As an example, I have been a practicing Catholic my whole life. I can remember, albeit shamefully now, times when I was on my way to church as a teenager or young adult and would bump into an acquaintance. They would ask me where I was going, but rather than tell the truth, out of fear of not being "cool," I would lie instead and say I was going somewhere other than church. At least the lie gave me something to pray about in church!

> *Be yourself; everyone else is already taken.*
> —Oscar Wilde

It seems so silly now, but I remember at the time being nervous that people might make fun of me for practicing my religion. This was a time when I should not have cared what other people thought. Fortunately, I grew out of that quickly after I reached my twenties, but it is a poignant example of how people, especially teenagers and young people, succumb to peer pressure and overvalue the opinions of others. This point, however, is a good segueway into my next concept: people generally aren't paying attention to you.

It might seem hard to believe, but in actuality people are too involved with their own lives to pay much mind to what you think, say, or do. That might be an overly cynical way of looking at the world, but it certainly has at least a modicum of truth—especially in today's age of social media. Everyone thinks they are the star of their own show, with the whole world watching them. The truth is, there are about eight billion people running around our planet, each of them the center of their own show. Even though we think people are paying attention to us, judging us, thinking about us, and so on, in actuality they too are just trying to get by from day to day just like us.

Of course, there are ways to get others' attention, by committing a heinous crime such as murder, rape, or pedophilia. Trust me, people will be talking about you then. But I am talking about the more personal and day-to-day things we dwell on and fret about because we think the world is watching us. A zit on our face, a bad hair day (or in my case, a no-hair day), a few extra pounds, or even a new romantic partner. What matters in all of these cases is how we feel about ourselves, and in the case of romance, how we feel about our partners. The zit will go away, your hair will tame eventually, pounds come and go, and so on.

Yet, despite the temporary nature of these "problems," we can truly get inside our own heads and let them ruin a day or even weeks for us. The real problem is that because we think that the second we step outside, everyone will be staring at the volcano on our face, or our recent weight gain, or the "bird's nest" on our heads, we let the negative self-talk make us feel bad *before* anything has actually happened. The sooner you learn to own these less than flattering sides of ourselves, while also realizing that the general public really doesn't care that much about what you look like, the sooner you can liberate yourself from self-destructive self-talk that may run through your head.

Sure, you think, *Maybe strangers don't care about what I look like or who I date, but what about my friends, family, coworkers? I am sure they may have a few choice words*. I absolutely understand this—friends, family, and close acquaintances certainly hold a higher regard in our minds. I grew up in a family in which you couldn't so much as mispronounce a word without at least three people pouncing to ridicule you. Not to mention if you tried to be adventurous in the realm of fashion, they would eat you alive. (Who says a preteen boy can't wear a crystal pendant if he wants to!) So, I certainly know what it's like to have that gauntlet of people who don't seem to let you get away with anything. This is understandable. These people are your tribe, and tribes do not handle ideas like "change" and "different" easily. They already have put you into a "box in their minds," so anything that deviates from those cubical confines becomes a threat to their system of order.

When people feel threatened, they tend to lash out or get defensive. This can take the form of teasing, mockery, and derogatory comments in a hope that we will back down and get back into the box we were placed. Now, sometimes, our friends and family do want the best for us, so it behooves us to listen to them. To a degree, there is an importance of fitting in with the caveat that we shouldn't lie about who we are or pretend that we are something we are not.

If you are thinking about making a change in your life, or trying something new, then make sure it's true to yourself and important to you. Perhaps it's a new piercing, a tattoo, a new style of clothing, a new career, or maybe a new partner. Regardless, you have to decide that once you do it, you're going to own it because it's who you are. It may help to think about why the change was important to you. An exercise like this will help fortify you against any negative remarks from the typical naysayers in your life. After you've decided that this action is important to you, and what you want to do, just remember that people will not care as much as you think they do. Again, there may be some talk up front, or a joke here and there, but after a few days or a week, things will return to normal.

Now, this chapter is not a carte blanche to "do whatever you want." Nor am I an advocate of "if it feels good, then do it." I am talking about making changes that you truly want to make. If the change you want to make is to start using recreational drugs or to start eating only fast food every day, then your family and friends will hopefully step in not to be "Debbie Downers," but because they love and care about you. In fact, if good friends don't say anything or if they encourage that behavior, then you probably need to reevaluate your friends. You should be able to make positive and meaningful decisions that are important to you. You want to be able to do what's best for you without worrying about what others think.

Let me illustrate further with a more personal example. As I mentioned earlier in the book, I was once engaged to a beautiful, wonderful woman, but things did not work out. I couldn't quite put my finger on what the problem was, so after our breakup, after a few months of soul-searching, healing, and picking up the pieces, I decided to date again. I went back to the old well of online dating, but wasn't having much luck. I just didn't seem that interested.

Around the same time, I had made friends with a male coworker whom we'll call Ryan, and we quickly hit it off. I couldn't quite explain it, but I loved spending time with him. Before long, it seemed like I was more interested in furthering a relationship with Ryan, than finding a new woman. Looking back, it was a definite wake-up call for me. As I pondered what it all meant, I could no longer deny a physical and sexual attraction that I had seldom felt before. I was exhilarated and at the same time terrified at the implications, however.

It was a fateful day in October 2017 when I started the process of admitting that I was gay. On one hand, it was absolutely liberating—it explained why my relationships with women never lasted and always seemed one-sided. But on the other hand, my mind raced with negative thoughts of what others would think. How would I explain this to my family, my friends, my coworkers? I was thirty-three years old at the time and had dated only women. How could I explain or defend what seemed like such a capricious change of heart? The process of coming out seemed exhilarating and insurmountable at the same time. It got to the point, however, where it no longer appeared to be a question of whether or not I was gay; it was more a question of what would people think of me.

Fortunately, I had decided I could no longer live my life based on the fear of what others might think of me. I chose to act instead. Slowly, over the course of six months or so, I came out to my family and friends. It was then that I realized that the worries and fears I had carried around inside me were just that: fear. My fears were pure fabrications and did not reflect reality. Not to say that coming out was easy. It wasn't. There were definitely some people in my life who were more quickly and easily accepting than others. However, none of my worst fears came to fruition. No one disowned me. No one joked about it or insulted me. In fact, I realized that people really aren't interested in my sex life (or that of others) as much as you would think.

I thought that there would be rumors or comments made at work or that people might look at me differently, but it turned out that people have better things to do. Of course, some people gossip and spread rumors, but at the end of the day, people are much too preoccupied with their own lives to worry about the minutiae of yours. I learned that it is human nature for us to think that we are all that other people think about, when in reality, everyone has their own drama to deal with. We definitely overestimate our own importance in other people's lives.

In summary, the last thing I would like to discuss is the topic of free speech. Unfortunately, there seems to be a dangerous trend in this country, and in the Western World generally, toward silencing speech. People are being told that they are not allowed to have an opinion on a topic because they might not be the right color, class, or gender. This is a dangerous conceit, and one that will take strength to overcome. We benefit from hearing the perspective of others, and silencing voices will not lead to solutions. So, if you see injustice or oppression, or something that is simply wrong, I encourage you to speak out and express your opinion. Do not fall into the trap of being told that "you're not allowed to have an opinion."

Anyone can have an opinion about anything. To be told otherwise is an attempt to intimidate you from expressing what some might deem an unauthorized or challenging view. Yet, it is times like these when it is more important than ever to be brave and not care what others think. You have a right to expression just as much as the next person. Your real friends will want to hear your ideas; they may debate you or disagree, but you are free to have your own opinions and express them. You should not pretend to agree with people out of fear that they "might not like you" if you speak up.

The other end of free speech is to listen. Listen to what other people are saying, and you may just learn from their experiences. Don't blindly believe everything you hear, of course. Rather, listen attentively and use your judgment to help decide what's true and what's false. Ask questions, explore topics further, and do your own research. By listening, you may well find out that people know things that you don't. This is how we grow as people. Listen especially to those with whom you disagree and those from different walks of life than you. Understand their arguments and hear where they are coming from. They may get you to change your mind, but they also will get you to think.

You will be forced to question what you believe and make sure it holds up to inquiry and debate. If not, go back and review your premises. Perhaps your opinions need adjustment. Regardless, this is why speech and debate are so important. Bad ideas do not hold up very long in the light of public scrutiny. We should be having more speech, not less. Be very wary when you hear people who wish to silence others.

The lessons I've learned are to be yourself, be humble, and not worry about what other people think. People aren't paying nearly as close attention as you think they are. Most people are simply focusing on getting through the day, or going from point A to point B, to notice everything and everyone else around them. So instead of worrying about what others might think about you or your actions, focus on being the best person you can be. Perhaps even reach out to a friend or family member who might be having a rougher time than you are. Offer a word of support to someone who is trying to better themselves so you can pay it forward.

Lastly, have courage and do not be afraid. Freedom of speech is one of our most precious gifts in this country, and it is one we should exercise the most forcefully. So get out there, be yourself, be brave, and don't always worry about what others will think.

# 12

# Time to Dump the Toxic Waste

*Nurture Your Real Relationships*

There are many ways in which we sabotage ourselves, but one of the most common is by surrounding ourselves with people who stifle our growth and improvement at best and seriously detract from our well-being at worst. Hollywood is replete with dramas and rom-coms about a protagonist who is clearly with the wrong person—someone who treats them like garbage. The plot then centers on the main character finally coming to the realization the right person for them has been under their nose the whole time (assuming you've made it this far through the movie).

It's become cliché at this point, but like most clichés there is an element of truth to them. Just think about your own life and recall the friendships that were not emotionally nourishing for you. This dynamic happens outside romantic relationships as well. Teenagers in particular are notorious for choosing the wrong group of friends, not to mention love interests as well. It is so common that you probably already have been able to think of several personal examples of such situations.

The question is, why is this so common? Each case has its own complexities, but the simple solution comes down to our innate desire as human beings to belong and to connect to others. Unfortunately, oftentimes the easiest way to do this is to have a partner or group of people who do not encourage our growth. Teenagers, not all of course, but many tend to fall into the "wrong crowd" because it's less challenging than being in the "right crowd." Let's say you are an average B student; you could choose to try to hang with the A students, where you will be at the bottom of the group, or you could choose to hang with the C students and be at the top. The A group might push you to study and work harder, take more credits, and join more clubs, which sounds like a lot of work. Or you can join the latter group of "friends," who make you feel smart, while at the same time only ask you to skip class and smoke pot from time to time. Although not everyone makes the poor decision, it is clear why falling into the wrong crowd can be tempting to someone who wants a group to fit into.

Finding a group or a tribe to belong to is a natural human desire. Few, if any, are truly happy as loners; we all want to avoid being seen as an outcast at any cost. Even as adults, we can succumb to the same poor decisions we had made in our teenage years. Unfortunately, it is not uncommon to see people with partners who physically or mentally abuse them or who are just downright deadbeats. Yet, despite all the evidence to the contrary, many will claim they still love or need such partners. The decision boils down to "my partner might not be perfect, but hey, at least I'm not alone!" Romantic relationships aside, adults still have the ability to pick the wrong friends as well.

The need to fit in or feel better about ourselves can cause us to pick friends to whom we may feel superior (thinner, smarter, or prettier), but these friends don't necessarily challenge us to be better people. On the other hand, we can choose relationships that we think elevate our status, such as befriending someone who is rich or attractive, because we think we will be seen as rich and attractive by association. All the while, that person is using us to feel better about themselves and could really care less about how we feel.

So clearly, there are many ways to get relationships wrong, but before we paint any more of a nihilistic view on friendship and romance, let's start delving into how to get things right. The first step is to recognize whether you are in a toxic relationship. Also, we must understand that any relationship we have with another is by definition an exchange.

Whether it's the clerk at the grocery store or a close confidant, any time we are interacting with someone to exchange money, ideas, emotions, or support, that interaction constitutes a relationship. A toxic relationship, however, is one in which you are generally giving more than you are getting, you are not growing or improving, or the other party involved does not necessarily want what is best for you. (Think of a loan shark or an unethical salesperson who is more interested in taking your money than in your well-being.) In a healthy relationship, on the other hand, you are at least getting back what you give; you are being kindly pushed and fostered to grow and improve. You genuinely feel that the others involved in your relationship want you to succeed.

With this in mind, think about your current closest relationships...with your partner, your family, or your best friends. Which category would you put them into, toxic or healthy? Of course we can all think of times when we fought with our spouse (like when he didn't agree that *Downton Abbey* is a great show even if most of the drama centers around whether the silverware will be polished in time for dinner—a real nail-biter!) or when our best friend hurts us (like when your friend stole your Malibu Barbie or dated your boyfriend behind your back), but I want you to think more long term. Over the course of your relationship with them, are they lifting you up or putting you down? Hopefully, it's the former, but if not, let's dive in further.

The easiest toxic relationships to spot are the ones in which you are either physically or mentally abused. These aren't necessarily the easiest ones to break, however, as the abuser is often a spouse, partner or a family member—someone on whom you have come to depend. First and foremost, you should never be in a relationship where your physical safety is in jeopardy. If that is the case, you need to seek help immediately, either from other friends or family, the police, domestic abuse support groups or hotlines. Even though each situation is unique, removing oneself from such a situation is not often as simple as getting up and leaving. Just know that you are not alone and that there is help out there for you. Support may vary by county and state; please contact your local health department or department of public services for more information.

Physical abuse is easy to recognize, but mental abuse can be more insidious and less visible. Is your relationship one in which you feel you are constantly put down verbally? Mental abuse can also take the form of constant belittling, intended to make you feel inferior, stupid, or unattractive. The goal here is for the dominant partner/friend to make the other party feel submissive and dependent. Clearly, there are obvious and direct examples of such behavior which include your partner blatantly telling you you're "fat and stupid" (that's a red flag, by the way), but be aware of the more insidious ways this can present. Dominance exerts itself in the form of someone who has complete financial control or someone who makes all the big (or even little) decisions.

Do you truly feel you are an equal partner with an equal say, or are you consistently overruled when it comes to how money is spent, where and what to eat, or how to spend your free time? Naturally, it is common in relationships for one person to be better with money or accounting—he or she handles financial responsibilities or balances the books. But that should not mean that you do not have a say in how money is spent. Similarly, some-one might be a better cook, but that should not mean that they are solely responsible for feeding the family (unless that person is truly happy to do so without objection). Ultimately, relationships are nuanced, and each one is different. However, in a healthy relationship each party should feel they have a voice and equal say in the day-to-day affairs. A toxic relationship is one in which one party repeatedly feels unheard, overruled, or belittled.

What about fighting? Does fighting mean you are clearly in a toxic relationship? The short answer is no, but it depends on how often you fight, and more importantly how you fight. Every couple fights. It is a natural outcome of two people cohabitating for each one to have their own thoughts, beliefs, and behaviors. However, the frequency of the fights, and their subject matter, can indicate whether the fights are normal or signals of a toxic relationship.

If you are fighting over every little thing (the tooth-paste cap, the dishes, the laundry, television programs, or what and where to eat), then that certainly is problematic, even if you are fighting the *right* way. (More on fighting the *right* way later in this chapter.) Life should not con-sist of daily battles between you two, and you will need to find workable solutions to meet each other halfway on issues in which you disagree. You both will have to cede some ground if the relationship is going to work. An example of a compromise would be deciding on a dishwashing schedule so that each one takes turns hav-ing the dishes done in a timely matter. Similarly, you can alternate who gets to pick where or what to eat or what to watch on television.

Although I mention solutions to these examples, I personally advise against resorting to turning your relationship into a series of transactions. ("I did the dishes yesterday, so you owe me the dishes today.") The better solution is to sit down and talk about what is important to you and why. Ideally, you can hopefully find common ground, but you also will have to pick your battles. Yes, leaving the cap off the toothpaste is annoying, but is it worth fighting over? Likewise, leaving clothes on the floor or dishes in the sink might not bother *you,* but if it bothers your partner, do you not love and respect them enough to tidy up after yourself?

Open up the dialogue and again decide what's important. Relationships are a give and take, and you both have to give in a little and let other things slide. At the end of the day, however, you might find that neither of you are willing to compromise, at which point you have to decide whether the rest of the relationship outweighs this point of contention. If you are a neat freak and your partner is a slob and neither of you are willing to budge, then you have to decide if the positive aspects of the rest of the relationship balance the fact that you will be doing all of the cleaning. It's not that a relationship like this *can't* work, but you truly would have to accept this aspect of the relationship and be sure that neither of you harbors resentment.

Furthermore, if you discover you can't find middle ground on daily, and arguably trivial matters, such as what television program to watch, where to go out, or what to eat, you might have to face the fact that you are not compatible. You might love this person or have incredible chemistry, but compatibility is just as important. Chemistry is the visceral, emotional response you have toward your partner. It is the sexual and physical attraction as well. It is also how you love their laugh or smile, or the way they pronounce or rather mispronounce a word, or any other of their idiosyncrasies. Chemistry is what most of us depend on in the beginning of the relationship. After all, you are not likely to date or get to know someone whom you do not find attractive or appealing.

Yet, chemistry only gets us so far. After a few weeks or months of a relationship, we are no longer simply doe-eyed in love, but rather are looking for something deeper with which to build a foundation for the future. This is where compatibility comes in.

Compatibility is the pragmatic portion of the relationship, the part that says "this can work." There are many ways in which to be compatible, but it comes down to sharing at least some of the same interests or behaviors. Do you both share similar values when it comes to religion/spirituality, career goals, housekeeping, politics, family planning, or geographical location? Do you have similar interests in types of books, movies, cuisine, vacations, sports, and fitness? As you can see, there are many facets to compatibility, and a successful couple need not agree on everything.

However, if you find there are more areas in which you differ than you agree, then you are certainly setting yourself up for conflict, perhaps even failure. Of course, not every category has equal weight either. You might both decide that your shared religion is the biggest value you both have, which in many cases can make up for the fact that you like different shows or cuisines. On the other hand, you might both be of the same political persuasion and share many other similar interests, but if one of you doesn't want children and the other does, that is going to be extremely difficult, if not impossible, to overcome. The point is, compatibility becomes critically important the longer the relationship goes on. Having a strong foundation in terms of compatibility is what allows the chemistry a couple shares to fill in whatever gaps a couple may have in their values or interests. If the gaps are too wide, however, no amount of chemistry can bridge them.

Okay, so back to the juicy part: fighting. Conflict is a normal and common part of any relationship. When conflict arises, each side readies to stand its ground, allowing conflict to quickly escalate to a fight. The question is, are you going to fight the right way or the wrong way? There are many wrong ways to fight, so let's go through a few of the classics. The most common way to fight incorrectly is by resorting to absolute statements ("you *always* do this" or "you *never* do that"). This is a bad strategy because absolute statements are (almost) never true. Furthermore, absolute statements do not allow for the possibility that someone could change. You are scolding them when you should be letting them know what you need or want from them instead.

The next mistake is to keep a scorecard and start bringing up issues from the past, or especially resurrecting issues that were supposed to have been resolved. Fights are not about scoring points or about using "credit" from prior arguments you might have "won." For instance, saying something like "Well, we get to do what I want tonight because you forgot about our anniversary last month" is neither a mature nor productive way to quarrel. Instead, it demonstrates your ability to hold a grudge and build hostility between you. Focus, rather, on the issue at hand without dwelling on fights from the past.

> *Life is made of ever so many partings welded together.*
> —Charles Dickens

Another big mistake people make is failing to listen. When you are arguing with your partner, take time to listen to what they are actually saying. Many people, instead of listening, are busy formulating their next rebuttal with which to club their opponent. How are you ever going to resolve a dispute if neither of you truly knows what the other is saying? The proper course of action here is to, "duh," actually listen to your partner! The way to ensure that you are doing this is to rephrase what your partner said back to them to make sure you understood it correctly.

For instance, "Okay, what I'm hearing you say is that you don't want to hang out with my friends tonight because you think they're incredibly dull and stupid." This then gives your partner the chance to confirm or correct what you think you heard. More importantly, however, it slows down the tempo of the disagreement so that instead of slinging arrows as quickly as possible, you now see each other as human beings with thoughts and feelings.

The last thing I would mention about fighting poorly is arguably the most important: avoid, at all costs, name-calling. Now it might seem harmless to hurl an insulting title at our partners in the heat of a dispute, but in fact, it can be a sign that your relationship is in real trouble. Calling someone a "fat cow," "stupid idiot," "a bitch," or even a "loser" in a fight sounds incredibly common, but it is also extremely damaging to the relationship.

When you name-call like this, what it demonstrates is some degree of contempt for the other person. You are beginning to relegate your mate to a category that is less than human. After you decide that someone is a bitch, scum, loser, worthless, or dirtbag, they no longer have the same worth or dignity in your mind that they once did. Yet this happens so frequently, likely because it prevents the need for further argument in our minds and, in a way, gives us a feeling of vindication. What more *would* you need to say to a "worthless loser" in order to win your point? Why waste your breath arguing any further?

Unfortunately, relationship research by renowned psychologist Dr. John Gottman demonstrates that this level of disdain and contempt is a frequent reason behind breakups and divorce. In fact, he describes such negative talk as one of the "four horsemen of divorce," and it is almost a point of no return. If you are to attempt to return, however, you must first decide and convince yourself that you do not truly believe these negative thoughts about your partner, and then resolve to never resort to such name-calling again.

To summarize the past few paragraphs, fighting is an unavoidable part of relationships, and it can end in disaster or in triumph. It is important to disagree the *right* way by truly listening to our partners: rephrase their arguments, avoid name-calling, do not rehash old disputes or keep score, and avoid absolute phrases. Fighting the right way can transform a dispute into an opportunity for growth and improvement. By listening and rephrasing our conversations while remaining civil, you can learn how and why the disagreement happened. This then opens you up to learning and understanding more about your partner and what is important to him or her.

Before moving on, I would also like to dispel a common myth that "you should never go to bed angry." I believe the sentiment of this statement is true in that you do not want to dwell on disagreements or let them fester. However, there are definitely times when a discussion should take place the next morning or at a later date. The two most common situations when a fight should be postponed is when either party is too tired or perhaps too intoxicated to have a reasonable conversation. The telltale signs of either are using a tone you wouldn't normally use, saying things you don't mean (name-calling), and, my personal favorite, talking in circles.

If you notice any of these signs it is perfectly reasonable, and recommended, to go to bed and wait until both of you are sober and hopefully more rested the next day to talk about the issue at hand. This can be difficult to do in the heat of the moment, so adopting this strategy early on is a good idea. Otherwise, remember that it takes two to tango, so resolve yourself to walk away from the argument and go sleep on the couch, in another room, or at a friend's house if need be. Trust me, you will have a far more productive and reasoned conversation in the morning.

Let's move on to platonic relationships such as those with family, friends, and peers. Family can often be a blessing, but certainly can be a curse as well. Our parents are not perfect, and neither are our siblings and relatives. Yet the bond of a common upbringing ties us all together. For many, family is a source of support, protection, and strength. Unfortunately, this is not always the case; families can be toxic to our growth and development, even as adults. The good news is that the situation doesn't have to remain this way.

Like in any relationship, the first step is to recognize whether your familial relationships are nurturing or toxic.

Does your family belittle you or, more commonly, make you feel less significant than another family member? Perhaps they are overly critical of any ideas or plans you have for the future. Do they accept your lifestyle and sexuality? (Assuming both are positive and productive? If they are critical of you being a prostitute to obtain money for heroin, then I am going to have to side with your family on that one.) The list could go on and on, but the bottom line is that you should feel that you have a place in your family and that your family is a source of love, respect, and support.

Remember, however, relationships are a two-way street, so you have to also make sure both to demand love, respect, and support, as well as act in a way that is worthy of those virtues. No adult is *entitled* to these responses from others and instead these responses must be earned. (Note: This does not apply to babies and young children who are entitled to unconditional love and support.) This book is directed toward an adolescent and adult audience, although precocious children are welcome to read it as well.

As mentioned, if you are the type that prefers to stay at home, sponging off your parents or other family, lying around, not looking for work, not contributing to the household, then you rightly deserve criticism and should not garner any respect. Like all adult relationships, you both get and give. So, make sure you are doing your part: helping out with the family, providing financial support when you can, working—either in the workforce or in the household. Be industrious, living each day to make your family a little better than the day before. Then you will be worthy of respect.

So what if you are doing the right things, but still feel you are not loved, respected, or supported? Well, then it is time to stand your ground and make your needs known. If, for example, your family does not approve of your partner, job, or lifestyle, then it is time to speak up and have them understand why these aspects of your life are important to you. Let it be known that you will not tolerate any disrespect toward them. The key is to delineate your situation to get them to understand and accept it, and from there they may just someday love, respect, and appreciate it. If your family truly loves you, they want you to be happy.

Often, when there seems to be discord in the family, it stems less from malice and more from misunderstanding. It is crucial to explain without arguing or battling. If you approach it as a debate, it will likely deteriorate into a battle. If you instead approach the matter as a discourse or explanation, staying cool and calm, you will likely be more successful in achieving understanding. It is important, though, that you make certain you feel strongly and are absolutely sure about what you are trying to explain and that you make it clear that you are not looking for debate or to be talked out of it. You are simply looking for some level of acceptance and understanding.

Naturally, whatever it is that you are trying to defend to your family, they will have some questions, counterpoints, or arguments of their own. It is important, pivotal even, to make sure they feel heard. This is an excellent time to remain calm and repeat their points back to them to ensure that you understand them correctly. This is your opportunity to allay any fears that they may have, address any concerns, and to assure them that what you are doing makes you happy, healthy, and productive. By remaining calm, standing your ground, and listening as well as speaking, it is possible for points of contention among family members to eventually resolve into places of love and acceptance.

So, what if you try to achieve understanding and despite your calm attempts you still have not engendered the acceptance for which you were hoping? The next step would be to agree to disagree or not to discuss it. For example, let's say one of your parents does not approve of your choice of career (they wanted you to be an engineer, but you chose to be a school teacher). If, despite your efforts, they continue to mock, sneer, or belittle you, or just simply disapprove, see if you can agree to not bring up the subject anymore. If you can, then take the relationship for what it is and do not push the issue.

However, if they continue to deride you for choices, then it might be time to limit your contact with them or find more neutral occasions to spend time with them (weddings, parties or other gatherings). The fact is that at some point you need to stand up for yourself and make it clear that you will not tolerate derision or hostility. Sometimes creating a little distance and setting boundaries opens doors to communication. It sets the tone, clarifying that if they want a relationship with you, then here is what you expect and where they can meet you.

Even though most of the preceding paragraphs have been told from the point of view from a son or daughter navigating relationships with parents and siblings, the same advice holds true for parents at well, albeit in a reverse sort of way. There are, unfortunately, plenty of instances where the children are the toxic aspect of a family's relationships with one another. Older children may abuse their parents, steal money from them, ridicule them, or otherwise take advantage of them. The situation is more difficult when your child is a minor because you are legally still responsible for them, but if you have a young adult in your life who is not giving you the respect you deserve, it is time for a change.

Again approach the situation calmly and explain what it is about their behavior that you will no longer tolerate. You are not debating or bargaining here; you are explaining. Define what behavior will be non-negotiable (physical or verbal abuse, abusing drugs or alcohol while living in your house, or playing video games all day while forgoing a career or education). Use this as an opportunity to express your love and concern for them, while outlining the changes in behavior that need to be made. Lastly, explain the consequences should their behavior not change (cutting them off financially, evicting them from the house, or severing ties with family). Here, I am emphasizing more drastic situations, but lower-level offenses (not cleaning their room, for instance) could involve a similar course of actions (naturally, with more fitting consequences—I am not suggesting you cut off ties with your child because they didn't clean their room!).

The point is to identify when the relationship with your child has become toxic, and then to demand what you will and will not accept. Furthermore, you must be stalwart in choosing to no longer enable your child, regardless of how painful it might be. If your child is stealing money from you, or worse, if you are giving them money that you know they are using for drugs, alcohol, or other maladaptive activities, then you need to be clear that you will no longer enable such behaviors. It's not that you don't love them anymore; it's because you love them. By continuing to support their self-destructive behaviors, you are complicit in their downward spiral. Your support is hurting them, and by setting rigid boundaries you are making it clear that you will not hurt someone you love. Allowing your children to sink will hopefully help them learn how to swim.

Family dynamics are extremely complicated, and many books have been written on the subject. I hope that this chapter gives a little guidance on where to begin and some advice for how to start thinking about and navigating your way through potentially toxic familial relationships. Before I draw this chapter to a close, let's next explore the ways in which our friends can actually be foes to our health and well-being.

Unlike familial relationships, which are forced upon us, when it comes to friendships we are at a considerable advantage in that we actually get to choose those with whom we associate. Why is it then that so many people fall into false friendships? As discussed earlier, many times we form friendships with people who make us *feel* better about ourselves, but do not in reality make us better people. We simply look better by comparison. We, ourselves, might not be the most thin, attractive, or smart person, but if we are thinner, smarter, or more attractive than a friend, we instantly get an ego boost.

The obvious problem here is that first, you are clearly using the other person, and second, you are surrounding yourself with such people who give you an excuse to not better yourself. Of course, in any relationship, one person is going to be superior in some aspect to the other person. However, I am not talking solely about just one friend you might have that you believe is generally inferior in some regard to you. I am referring more generally to the pattern of friendships you make. Do you befriend people who inspire you and wish for you to be better? Or do you prefer people who justify your maintenance of the status quo?

I talked earlier about how common this is for teenagers. For example, the average B student who prefers to associate with the C students to absolve him from any effort to try harder. After all, he is leading his peer group. However, had he chosen to strive to be among the A students he just might be able to pull himself up there as well. The comfort we get from associating with those beneath us persists through adulthood as well. For instance, we can either recall or imagine a wealthy person, who flaunts their affuence to their friends, who are not wealthy, and in this case the pathology could work both ways. The rich person gets a boost from boasting his wealth to friends who are not as well off, while the friends of more modest means might enjoy associating with the rich and famous and eating the crumbs that fall off the table.

Please note: I am not saying rich people can't be friends with poor people or that fat people can't be friends with thin people without having an ulterior motive. I only use these as examples of ways in which the friends we keep might be kept for the wrong reasons.

There are more insidious ways that friendships can be toxic, aside from the examples I've mentioned. Do you feel comfortable speaking your mind to your friends, or are you afraid that they might leave you if you don't toe the line? Can you have an honest debate or discussion with your friends without it erupting into all-out war? Can you give and receive honest feedback from your peers? Do you have at least one or two people in your lives whom you could count on if your car broke down, or you were out of work, or even to pick you up from the airport if needed? These are just a few of many questions we could ask ourselves to determine the integrity of the friendship. If the answer was no to any of these, you probably need to look for better friends. Of course, there are degrees of friendships, and you wouldn't depend on your friendly work acquaintance the same way you would your best friend from childhood. But the point is that we need at least one or two solid friendships in which we can truly be ourselves, say what we think, give and receive honest feedback.

It is my belief that one of the best metrics of a relationship is being able to speak freely to the other person without reprisal. In today's day and age of political polarization and countless controversial issues, being able to speak out without reprisals is in short supply. This is especially the case when we count media such as Twitter and Facebook; these forums allow everyone to become an instant pundit, and reason does not always rule the day. Do you have friends with whom you can disagree about something, but you can discuss it openly? Or does every disagreement devolve into a battle with personal attacks? Do you find that you frequently have to bite your tongue around your friends, lest they find out that you don't agree with their views? As discussed earlier, if someone is your real friend, you shouldn't have to pretend to be something you're not. You should be able to speak plainly to your true friends without worrying about what they might think. Naturally, there are times when we do have to go along to get along, such as in the workplace, but when it comes to the people who really matter to you in your life, you should have no need to hide your true self.

So, take an inventory of your friends and relationships. Do they inspire you to be better than you were yesterday, or do they provide a convenient excuse to maintain the status quo? For each close friend you have, I want you to be able to point to at least one trait about them that you admire and wish you had. Do you have close friends with whom you can speak without false pretense? Do your friends truly want the best for you and want to see you succeed? If the answer is *no* to any of these, then you need to seriously look at the relationship and decide whether it is true or toxic. If your friends don't inspire you to improve, don't give you the comfort to speak freely, and wouldn't be there for you in an emergency, it is time to dump the waste and move on.

I have covered a lot in this chapter, and more could certainly be said. I hope that this discussion empowers you to take charge of your relationships whether they be romantic, familial, or friendly. The relationships we have with others in our lives are one of the most valuable parts of the human experience. It is up to us to act wisely and ensure that the people in our lives lift us up rather than drag us down. Likewise, we too must behave in ways worthy of love and respect and be a source of support for others. In doing so, we can fully satisfy the human need for love and companionship, and we can help others do the same.

# 13

# Religion and Spirituality

*There's Gotta Be More to Life Than This!*

As time and culture move forward, people, especially in the Western world, are becoming increasingly more secular—not concerned with religion or church. Many look to science to answer the questions once reserved for religion. They may now consider religion, and even God, obsolete. Yet is this truly the case?

Sure, through scientific inquiry, great minds have unraveled quite a few of the many phenomena formerly deemed mysteries by ancient man. We no longer believe that lightning is anger from the gods, nor that seasons change because of the unfolding dramas coming from heaven. However, we still have not answered so many of the deeper questions. What is the meaning of life? Is there a greater purpose to our actions? Who, if anyone, created this universe, and why? Does the soul exist, and what happens to it when we die? Although we are becoming increasingly more confident that science will eventually answer any question we ask, it is my opinion that there will always be a place for faith in our lives.

Before we go further, a few disclaimers. This is not a book about theology, nor am I trying to argue for one religion or spiritual practice over another. I am a practicing Roman Catholic, so some of my views will invariably be shaped through that lens. I mention this so as to be

138

upfront about any potential biases you may perceive. I will do my best to be as general as possible, however, and not push one religion over another. Furthermore, I will mention the term "God" throughout this chapter for the sake of simplicity (or at least as simple as one can futilely attempt to make "God" be). Please know that for the sake of generality you can substitute whatever term you are more comfortable with (creator, lord, nature, spirit, or cosmos) as long as it refers to an idea of something bigger than ourselves, or the sense of some sort of cosmic ruler, judge, or creator.

Moving along, it is my belief that mankind has an eternal thirst for the divine. Science, and the technology it has fostered, has done so much to make our lives better and easier, but they can never replace the need we as people feel to connect to each other and to something or someone bigger than ourselves. Yet, increasingly, God has been chased out of both the public and personal square. Religion and spirituality are hardly represented in pop culture, and people who practice religion are often portrayed as "backward." It is increasingly impressed upon us that talking about God, praying, or going to religious services is at best "not cool," and at worst taboo. Our culture even bends over backward to not mention the "G-word." As an example, I saw a comedic television show the other day in which Christmas was referred to as "Santa Claus's birthday" (spoiler alert: it's not!). At the same time, it seems you can see just about anything else on television or Internet streaming services: have sex, run a meth lab, launder money for drug cartels, and of course kill people as needed should they conflict with your interests.

Now, I am not advocating for theocracy or censorship. I only wanted to illustrate a point as to how far the pendulum has swung away from a country that openly talked and debated about God and the spiritual world in the public square to one in which you can virtually do anything *but* mention God. Moreover, we have been fed a diet that is spiritually quite poor. Citing these examples, we have been led to believe that more sex is better, more money is better, and human lives have worth only if they are not in your way. Again, I am not campaigning to censor drugs, sex, or violence from the entertainment industry; however, I do believe that when such messages are not balanced by a search for more eternal truths such as those that religion or spirituality provides, the results are a more depressed, cynical, and nihilistic society—one that rejects morality and religion, believing that life has no meaning.

> *The best remedy for those who are afraid, lonely or unhappy is to go outside, somewhere they can be quiet, alone with the heavens, nature, and God. Because only then does one feel that all is as it should be.*
>
> —Anne Frank

The evidence is all around us, particularly so during the COVID-19 pandemic. Efforts to mitigate the virus have caused many governments to forcefully isolate their citizens from one another and also from God. Although there were many places you *could* go during the pandemic (Wal-mart, Home Depot, and liquor stores), places of worship were *not* among them. People were forced out of work, and many of those who still had their jobs could no longer personally interact with their coworkers. Kids were kept out of school and away from developing with their peers. Those who still practiced a religion were prevented from doing so publicly.

The result: rising rates of alcohol use, domestic violence, depression, and thoughts of suicide. There are many reasons for these matters, and I think we can recognize two things. First, there is hubris in thinking we can use technology (in the form of web-based learning and Zoom meetings) to replace the fundamental human need for personal interaction and physical touch. Second, humans cannot exist in a vacuum, and we do not do well when deprived of the ability to connect with something bigger than ourselves, whether that is simply the natural world or the divine.

Speaking of technology, we live in a world where almost everything is at our fingertips. Most people, at least in the United States, can push a button and instantly watch whatever movie they want, listen to any song they choose, or order any type of cuisine they wish. If they want a new toy or clothing, they can order these as well and have it at their doorstep often no later than tomorrow. It is instant gratification like we have never seen before. Yet this "speed" comes at a cost. We have become more impatient, less restrained, and feel more entitled than ever before. Virtues such as temperance, patience, and chastity have gone by the wayside. Arguably, these virtues were in decline before the Internet, but the hyper-connectedness of the modern world makes them all too easy to cast off. I admit, I too love the ease and conveniences today's technology offers; however without the timeless truths and wisdom of religion and spirituality to counterbalance them, it is easy to see how a culture could deteriorate.

As I've stressed throughout this book, we humans yearn for something more than our basic physical needs. With advancements in our understanding of chemistry and biology, there are some who argue that science is all we need. They insist that all of the complexity, uniqueness, and individuality present in every human being can be boiled down to the interaction of chemical reactions and physical processes. They argue that there is no such thing as free will, but rather every decision we make is simply the result of neurons firing in our brains—a response to predictable chemical reactions.

In essence, we are no longer divinely inspired beings made in the image of an omnipotent creator, but instead mere clumps of molecules destined to whatever outcomes result from the dictations of organic chemistry. Romantic, huh? It is no wonder that once untethered from the moorings of a deeper plan or larger meaning, many people have turned to an "anything goes" attitude and, unsurprisingly, have attempted to alter those chemical reactions in our brain with pharmaceuticals and illicit drugs.

It is truly fascinating the breakthroughs and advancements that have been made in understanding human biochemistry, and this knowledge can be used to improve the human condition. However, I argue that it is a mistake to reduce humanity to a jumble of molecules and electrochemical interactions without any higher purpose. The reason I feel that way, aside from already having discussed how dangerous such a deconstructionist viewpoint can be, is that the more we learn about the natural world, the more apparent it seems to be that there must have been some sort of higher design in its creation. If there is a design, then this leads many to search for the possibility of a designer, whether you wish to call that designer "God" or use some other term.

As a medical doctor with a bachelor's in mechanical engineering, I have had to undergo many years of study in the natural sciences—physics, chemistry, and biology, to name a few. While studying the sciences can certainly have a tendency to make one more atheistic, my education seems to have had the opposite effect. The more I learned about the natural world, the more clear it seemed to me that there was such beauty in it and an apparent design. I remember being a freshman engineering student going through the grueling Physics I and II offered by my university, when I was struck by two almost identical equations (in form, anyway) that described two of the most fundamental forces in our universe: gravity and electromagnetism—a concept that deals with the force that occurs between electrically charged particles.

These two laws explain how the planets revolve around their stars, why apples fall to the ground, and why a battery works. It amazed me at a young age how two such disparate forces could be described by virtually identical equations. In my opinion that points to the idea of someone bigger out there who had a design in mind. Of course, there are plenty of very complicated equations in physics and chemistry, but to have such simplicity and consistency in such fundamental forces still amazes me to this day. To me, it reinforces the idea that there is a plan or a purpose to the universe. Consequently, I believe we all have an innate desire to discover that purpose.

I mention religion in this book only because I personally feel strongly that having a God, spirit, creator, or other overarching purpose in your life is pivotal to mental health, but there is also scientific evidence to support this claim. In a recent Pew Research study, religiously active people scored higher than their nonreligious peers in terms of overall happiness; they are also more likely to participate in other community organizations and even tend to vote more in elections. The reasons for these findings are important. I believe that believing in a higher purpose gives meaning to your life. You become a part of something and are no longer just going through a meaningless existence only to die an insignificant death. In the Christian tradition, for example, we believe the meaning of life is to seek to know and have a relationship with God. Other religions or traditions may have different goals, but the result is the same: to focus and give purpose to your life. Religion aside, your higher purpose could be simply to help your fellow man or to preserve the environment, and I suspect the benefits will be the same.

Another aspect of religion I find particularly helpful in our mental health is the structure it provides. There is wisdom in rituals, which is why our ancestors established them. To take time out of every day or once a week to focus on something higher, something more spiritual and eternal, helps to center ourselves and create perspective. All of a sudden, whatever was worrying you that day (overdue bills, an argument with your spouse, the show *Friends* being taken off Netflix) seems to fall by the wayside as you focus on the bigger mysteries of life.

As a Catholic, I attend Mass every Sunday (admittedly, once in a blue moon I will miss a Sunday because of travel or work). I will not pretend that I always want to go church on a given day or that when I am at church, there aren't times when I am counting down the minutes until Mass is over. However, regardless of my level of commitment or engagement that particular day, I absolutely *never* leave Mass feeling worse than before I arrived. I always find it cleansing, focusing, cathartic, and simply soul-satisfying. Furthermore, it grounds me to the end of one week and the start of another. Whatever stress was going on in my life, or whatever crazy work schedule I am on, I am forced to pause for a breath while I go to church. Everything else can wait one hour on Sunday while I reconnect. No phones, no television, no news, no Internet: just me and God while the rest of the world stops. I hope you are starting to see the wisdom in this ritual.

I am not trying to push Christianity on anyone, so if church is not for you, then what about setting aside a non-negotiable time each day or week to meditate? If you prefer something more active, try going for a quiet walk for thirty to sixty minutes. Let yourself mentally wander. Whatever you choose to do, the goal is to quiet your mind and focus on the bigger picture of life and the universe. Make it a ritual, a time in your day or week that is set aside for this purpose. Going to church to celebrate Mass is a good example because it happens every Sunday (so I can't just push it off to another day). So, if you rather do your own form of meditation, reflection, or worship, I encourage you to try to create a consistent time and stick to it.

Another aspect of religion or spirituality is the idea of cleansing. In the Catholic tradition, we have a whole season just before Easter called Lent that is dedicated to just that, cleansing. This is performed through acts of prayer, fasting, and almsgiving, with a requirement to attend confession at least once, if you have not done so yet within the year. Other faith traditions have similar traditions, and you don't have to belong to any faith to still practice these acts of penance.

As another example, fasting is a great way to center yourself and nurture a spirit of gratitude for how fortunate most of us are here in the West with an abundance of food. It hopefully instills a spirit of generosity toward those who have no choice but to go without food for hours or days at a time. Furthermore, it teaches you to be mindful of your food and to learn to both appreciate and never take for granted the act of eating.

The act of confession might be a little harder to swallow for some, but similarly there is wisdom in this ritual. In the Catholic faith, the act of confession is performed by sitting with a priest either face to face or anonymously through a screen (like you've probably seen in movies), and confessing any and all major and even minor sins. The priest then absolves you of your sins and may have you say some prayer or perform an act of penance (such as fasting, or an act of charity). I realize this act of confession is a lot to swallow for the average person. I am not asking you to believe or perform everything I just described. However, I do feel that anyone of any or no faith can benefit from coming clean with their sins, failures, or wrongdoings.

Whether you confess out loud to another person or quietly to yourself, you are acknowledging ways in which you can improve; perhaps you'll feel the need to make amends with someone. This fosters an attitude of humility, which seems to be more and more lacking in a culture that increasingly thinks the world revolves around them. I encourage you to try some form of confession and open yourself to the healing that accompanies it.

Prayer and meditation are probably the most familiar, most common forms of ritual, but they can also be the most difficult. Prayer, for example, can take the form of "God, please do *this* for me" or "I am sorry for doing *that*." Even though this type of prayer is important, and acceptable, meditative prayer is where the real benefit lies. In meditation, and meditative prayer, you are simply quieting the mind and silencing the noise of the everyday world. In doing so, you open yourself up to a connection with something deeper.

In religious prayer, of course, that deeper something is communication with God, but for others it might simply be connecting with nature, or with your own mind, or creating a deeper sense of self. When I personally practice this type of prayer, I try to quiet my thoughts as I listen for any inspiration. No, I don't hear a loud booming voice saying, "Maxwell, I am your Father," but I do feel a connectedness with something bigger. On a subconscious level I am transformed, even if just in a small way. Even outside of religion, experienced meditators probably would voice something similarly transcendent. Now, I would not claim to be good at this type of meditation, and it is more difficult than it seems. But I do recommend you try it consistently for a few weeks and, with practice, I believe you too will feel the benefits of connecting to something on a higher level.

Lastly, almsgiving and charity round out our ability to atone for transgressions while focusing on something bigger than ourselves. By giving of your time, money, possessions, or abilities, you are acknowledging that there is more to life than just you. This instills a spirit of gratitude for all that you do have, while at the same time creating perspective for your problems, which may seem a little more trivial in light of the plight of others.

For those who have needs that are not being met, your helping them can allow them to experience gratitude. At the same time, when we are charitable toward others, we also can learn to be charitable toward ourselves. A priest explained this to me during confession a few years back. I never thought about applying charity inward. However, he talked about how we can often give such grace and aid to other people, but we fail to give it to ourselves. After reflecting on it, I realized how true it is that we can so easily beat ourselves up for our failures and shortcomings, while at the same time console a friend or family member for similar, or even worse, transgressions.

Thus, charity, along with a confession of some sort, can work hand in hand to improve our mental health and free us from the negative aspects of our past. Just like everything we talked about in this book, you don't have to go out and be Mother Teresa on day one. Why don't you start small and see where you can donate a little time or money on a regular basis to help those who are less fortunate? Volunteering at a soup kitchen, a church, or a nursing home is easy and a common way to get started. I believe once you do, you will open yourself to the healing that comes with charity toward others and yourself.

I know talking about things like God and religion can be off-putting or controversial to some. I hope that you didn't find that to be the case and that regardless of your beliefs you were able to take something away from this chapter. Studies do show that those who engage in religious practice or meditation live longer and happier lives than those who don't. I hope that you are inspired to explore what benefits religion and spirituality can add to your life.

# 14

# Gratitude

*Stop Looking for What's Missing*

Most of us have heard the phrase "Count your blessings!" numerous times—usually from a wise, elder family member. In reaction, we might have rolled our eyes or politely nodded our heads out of respect, not truly internalizing the wisdom of such a simple phrase. Yet, the happiest among us are those who do exactly that, count their blessings. Think about it: it is impossible to be both unhappy and grateful at the same time. Surprisingly, so many of us opt to be the former rather than the latter. Why is that?

There are many reasons, but chief among them is the draw to have a "victimhood" mentality, as well as the constant onslaught of information we receive each day via Facebook and Instagram. We tend to believe that everyone else's lives seem better than ours. Both forces combine together to ensnare us into dividing ourselves into the haves and the have-nots. In this chapter, let's delve deeper into these problems, and then go about the work of solving them.

Western culture, particularly in the United States, is making it increasingly more attractive to identify yourself as a victim. It is easy to see why. If you can find a way to blame something or someone else for your status in life, you absolve yourself from all guilt and responsibility. It is

Gratitude

a devil's bargain, though; because although you no longer carry any guilt, you are also neutered from any agency or control over your own life. Quite simply, life is something that "happens to you," rather than you shaping your own destiny. Naturally, I am not arguing that there aren't real victims of true injustice. What I am arguing is that most of the negative outcomes in our lives that we perceive as injustice are actually within our control.

This victimhood can start at an early age. When a student performs poorly in a class or on a test, they are quick to offer excuses for their performance. "I didn't have enough time," "The questions were unfair," or as my sister used to claim, "My teachers were drunk." Although sometimes there are bad tests or drunk teachers, it is more likely that the student did not prepare adequately for the exam. As we get older, we can carry these excuses with us, albeit they make take a more serious form. If we get passed up for a job or promotion, we may cry that we were not selected because of racism or sexism. If we can't make our mortgage or rent, we may insist that the rates are unfair or that the banks are out to get us. Nowadays, if we perceive any unjust disparity in our lives the "bogeyman du jour" is to blame "the system."

To be clear, there is and has been true systemic injustice both in this country and throughout the world. However, blaming things outside of our control has become increasingly popular, even though we, in America at least, live in one of the most free and just societies in human history. Disparity will always exist, and some people are born with more privileges than others. Being born into a loving two-parent household, having wealth, and living in a low-crime neighborhood are all privileges. However, just because you didn't have any or all of those things does not mean you are a perpetual victim who can never overcome a lower hand in life.

Privileged or not, your life comes down to choices, *your* choices. Newspapers and tabloids are replete with

149

stories of people who were born to privilege only to squander their wealth and end up destitute. Conversely, there are plenty of people who, despite having very little to start with, were able to take control of their lives and rise to prominence in a number of fields—academics, business, politics, and sports.

Victims do exist, and tragedy does befall us from time to time. However, if you adopt a perpetual victimhood mentality, then you create a self-fulfilling prophecy. If you believe that you can't improve your lot in life because something or someone is holding you back, then you will convince yourself of the futility of even trying to succeed. If instead, you decide that despite what may have happened to you that you are going to continue to work to be better tomorrow than you are today. Only then will you find that you truly can improve your lot in life. So, begin today by ditching your victimhood and take control of your life.

*Happiness resides not in possessions and not in gold,*
*the feeling of happiness dwells in the soul*
—Democritus

Whatever the situation you wish to improve: your job, your health, your finances, or your relationships, instead of asking "What happened that got me here?" ask "What did *I* do to get here, and what can *I* do to get out?" By changing from the passive tense of "happened to me" to the active voice of "can I do," we empower ourselves to take agency and control over our lives. We cannot control what others do or the natural calamities that may befall us, but we can control how we respond.

It may sound silly, simplistic, or too easy, but by changing your mentality and reminding yourself that "I am not a victim," you can truly change your life. As a personal example, I went through a period of malaise and lack of mental energy early in my career after finishing my residency. I was working a lot in the emergency room, which if you watch television would have you believe I was having the time of my life, cracking people's chests open and saving lives with CPR. Yet I found my work became mundane.

I had jumped through all the hoops of medical school and residency, climbed all the ladders, and now that I had made it, I felt unfulfilled. I myself even started to adopt a victim mentality. I languished over how I felt trapped in the job because I needed to pay back my hefty student loans and justify in my mind spending more than seven years of my life in school and training to become a doctor. One day, dwelling on my perceived misfortune I woke up and realized that I am in no way a victim. I am not trapped in a job. I am *choosing* to be in this job. I might not always love it, but no one is forcing me to do it. I could quit tomorrow and find another job. I could cut back on hours and take a little longer to pay off my loans. Or, if I really wanted, I could find a way to work part-time and go back to school or train for another job altogether.

The point is that I started to believe I was a victim. stuck in a system of medical education and debt, and I suffered from the accompanying unhappiness that such a mentality brings. Simply by changing my attitude and approaching my work from a position of personal choice and agency, I nurtured a spirit of gratitude for my job and made myself a much happier person. I realized the only person who made me feel trapped was myself. Several years later, I am now in the same job and love it, and I am so grateful to be able to do the work that I do.

Now, I am sure some of you are rolling your eyes and trying to hold back the tears for my "poor doctor" story, knowing that you have bigger issues than merely feeling trapped in your job. The point of the story, however, is how dangerous and powerful a victimhood mentality can be in oppressing us and preventing our happiness. Much of life, depending on how we look at it, can be a source of misery or merriment. It all depends on our attitude.

Now, I want you to think about your own life situations in which you felt trapped, or you believe that you are a victim. Are you in a loveless relationship? Think about ways that *you* can fix it (counseling, finding a new partner, moving to a new town). Are you unhappy about your weight or health? Start strategizing how *you* can improve it (eating better, exercising, seeing your doctor, quitting smoking or drinking). Hate your job? Then come up with a plan that you will execute (talking to your boss, going back to school, looking for a new job). I talked earlier in the book about executing plans and not making excuses, so this might be a good time to reread that section. The point of this chapter is to remove the blame from "the system" and put the responsibility, and power, back onto *you*.

We have already touched on the role platforms such as Facebook and Instagram can play in our unhappiness, but it bears repeating in this chapter as well. Social media, while being a great way to stay connected to a lot of people, certainly can foster an attitude of envy rather than one of gratitude. As I explained earlier, when we use these apps, we are instantly inundated with photos of others, seemingly living their lives better than we live our own. Rather than being grateful for all that is going right in your life, it is all too tempting to look longingly at the fortune of others and wonder why that can't be us. We get glimpses of just the highest points of other people's lives, and we start to wonder what we are doing wrong. Of course, this is nonsensical thinking, and we must remind ourselves that for every amazing vacation photo a friend posts online, there were likely countless hours of hard work at a job to pay for those experiences.

Naturally, the point is not that we should wish that other people have challenges and setbacks to counteract the perfect moments captured in their online posts, but rather to remind ourselves that everyone is human and no one's life is perfect all the time. We all have moments of pain, loneliness, regret, and guilt; however, pictures that capture these moments usually don't make it onto Facebook.

Even bigger than social media is the knack we humans have for focusing on what's missing or wrong in our lives. We have an incredible ability to find flaws in every aspect of our lives. Much like how when you notice a stain on your shirt, suddenly that is *all* you see. We no longer appreciate how fine the rest of the garment is because of the stain; the entire shirt is now ruined. We apply a similar lens to much of our lives. Instead of savoring and appreciating how wonderful our lives are, we focus in on what is missing. Psychologists refer to this as "Missing Tile Syndrome." The name derives from imaging a beautiful tile mosaic floor that appears almost perfect except there is one small tile missing. Now, instead of admiring the beauty and intricacy of the design, all you can focus on is missing tile. The other 99 percent of the tiles might be in perfect shape and still give the impression that the designer was trying to convey; however, it is all for naught now that its beauty is marred by the absence of one tile.

This example might seem a little extreme, but it is a perfect example of how easily we can view our glass as half empty rather than half full. For instance, we might look at our homes and notice that the walls need to be repainted or the roof needs to be redone and begin to feel sorry for ourselves, wishing we could have a house as nice as the neighbor's. All the while not realizing that although the house may need some work, it still has a beautiful garden and a recently remodeled kitchen. By focusing on what is wrong, we rob ourselves of the joy present in all that is right. This applies to both material things as well as our relationships. Maybe your husband isn't a supermodel and sometimes forgets to put the toilet seat down, but that doesn't cancel the way he surprises you with flowers or simply makes you feel loved. Bottom line, nothing in life is perfect. We can choose to make ourselves miserable by focusing on what's missing, or we can find happiness by fostering some gratitude. That is not to say that we shouldn't try to improve ourselves or our lives, but we should approach such improvements with a sense of gratitude rather than disappointment or envy.

So, this sounds great, but how do we put it into practice? Well, as your grandma would have likely put it, "count your blessings." Although this sounds simple, almost too easy, just like any good habit, it takes work. In fact, I bet you will find that when you are in a rut of negativity, it can be extremely difficult to try to focus on the positive, especially if you are out of practice. I recommend starting with the biggest things that are easy to feel grateful for, so much so that we might even take them for granted.

At the top of my list would be the love from parents, my health, a loving partner, a safe home, a warm bed, two loving, if not mischievous, dogs, a steady job, my faith and the love of God, a reliable car, reliable friends and family, and even my proximity to multiple Trader Joe's stores. I came up with this list in less than a minute, and I bet that you can do the same. I am sure I could come up with twice as many with just a few more minutes of thought and reflection. If you are just starting to form these kinds of habits, this type of activity may feel a little strange for you, but it's okay to write down your list quickly and refer to it when you are feeling down. Whatever it is that is getting you down will likely come into perspective when stacked against a list of the things for which you are truly grateful. It really is a simple process, but it does take a conscious effort to become natural. Remember, it is impossible to be unhappy and grateful at the same time.

Lastly, I would like to talk to you about charity. When we give to others our time, energy, or money, we are, in a way, expressing gratitude for all that we have as well as our ability to share. I am sure I don't need to lecture you on how charity is a good thing, but it is an act of giving thanks for how fortunate we are and it creates perspective for us when we alleviate the plight of others. Come to think of it, it reminds me of another grandparent-type saying that usually follows the phrase "count your blessings," and that is that "things could always be worse." In a way, it may seem like a negative way to look at the world, but there is wisdom in the cliché. At the heart of this phrase is the creation of perspective. A little perspective goes a long way in securing your happiness.

I can remember not too long ago that I was stressing about planning a wedding amid the COVID pandemic. I remember at the time feeling plagued by a slew of negative responses to our invitations. (Many guests were still fearful of travel.) I could easily have succumbed to the negativity and moaned about what a failure the event would be, but instead I chose to count my blessings. We are blessed to still have a sizable amount of people who will make it to the big day, and we have such an incredible venue staffed with such great people who will make sure that the day is a success.

Next comes a little perspective. As I stress about the wedding I am forced to think about those who have lost loved ones from COVID, those who have lost their homes to recent fires and hurricanes, and of course those who have lost their livelihoods from lockdowns and civil unrest. All of a sudden, the diminution of my guest list did not seem like the biggest problem in the world. The ills that befall us are not the most pleasant to think about, but it does force me to refocus on the lack of magnitude of my problems at the moment.

Interestingly, I learned that charity does not apply only to others, but also to ourselves. I learned this while I was at confession of all places. Instead of being castigated by the priest for my proclaimed sins, he offered this pearl

155

of wisdom: "We must be charitable to ourselves." What he meant, of course, was that we must not be so hard on ourselves to the point of self-flagellation.

I know that I, like many people, can be my own worst critic, when instead there are times that I simply need to cut myself some slack. Rather than dwell on my perceived failures and shortcomings, being charitable to everyone, including myself, means giving myself a break. This comes with the caveat that I am also trying each and every day to be a better person than I was the day before.

What comes to mind for me are the times where I said or did the wrong thing, ate or drank too much, didn't get enough sleep, didn't prepare enough, and the list could go on. Rather than beat myself up for having done the wrong thing, I can adopt a spirit of charity and forgiveness toward myself, with the resolution to be better today. Remember this the next time you fall into a pit of self-despair.

In closing, I hope this chapter has given you a lot to think about. Namely, that you are not a perpetual victim and are absolutely in control of your life. Furthermore, be grateful for all that you have and let that gratitude be the foundation of your happiness. Do not let social media or envy of your neighbors prevent you from seeing and appreciating all that is going right in your life. We can always strive to be better, but let us take time to enjoy the good we have today. Be charitable to yourself and to others so that you nurture and share the gratitude you have for all that is good about you.

# 15

# Challenge Yourself

## The Struggle Is Real

It is human nature to avoid struggle, conflict, and stress. We all search from time to time to take the so-called easy way out. It is understandable, of course, from the perspective of our hunter-gatherer, and even our more modern, ancestors. For them, life was a constant struggle. They had to work tirelessly to find their next meal, maintain their shelter, and there was no Uber or Lyft to transport them.

In fact, up until the last century, life was "nasty, brutish, and short," according to Thomas Hobbes's influential work on political philosophy *The Leviathan*. It is only thanks to the advancements in medicine and technology with the advent of antibiotics, automobiles, and computers that our lives have become infinitely more convenient and arguably stress-free (I say that with a grain of salt; otherwise I wouldn't feel the need to write this book!)

Yet, in the absence of having to struggle for our mere existence, we have been left with voids to fill. Humans have an innate *need* to struggle. We do not do well being left to our own devices without any goals or tasks on the horizon. Once again, your grandmother was right: idle hands are the devil's playground. You have probably noticed this yourself. In hindsight, working toward a goal is often more satisfying than achieving the goal itself.

When you look back at some of your accomplishments, you may remember all the countless hours of work you put in, the sleepless nights, and the many cups of coffee. Of course, achieving the goal is wonderful too, but the elation is often short-lived. I don't often quote Miley Cyrus, but when she isn't making inappropriate gestures with a giant foam finger, she sometimes lets out a nugget of wisdom: "It's the climb."

In other words, it's not being at the top that we relish; it's the process of getting there. I, too, have experienced this, as I mentioned earlier in the book. I remember how exhilarating (okay, exhilarating in a "painful" sort of way) it was to work my way through pre-med, then into and through medical school and residency. Each week or month would be filled with a new milestone: completing organic chemistry, passing the MCAT (the medical school entrance exam), getting into medical school, passing my boards, graduation, and then finally acceptance and completion of my residency.

There were even more steps than that, but you get the idea. Even just writing about it now brings a smile to my face as I remember opening my first medical school acceptance letter and jumping with joy. I remember how pleased I was after interviewing for my ultimate residency spot; I was so excited for what the future had in store for me. Finally, I recall how incredible it was to graduate from residency filled with hope and enthusiasm for my new life as an attending physician in Dallas, Texas.

Then, after a few months of working as an attending physician, I started to feel a certain weariness. There were no more milestones, no more graduations, no "hills" left to climb. It began to feel empty, with a kind of "This is it?" feeling. I had been working toward this moment for the past ten years. I was at the point of getting off the "medical education treadmill." I realized that I, rather we all, need something to work toward in our lives to maintain our happiness.

Perhaps you have felt this way before as well. You have your life all together; maybe you have a spouse, kids, home, and car. Then you begin to feel like you're just coasting...not moving forward toward a goal.

Without challenges, life can start to feel like the classic 1990s movie *Groundhog Day*—each day feeling like a repeat of the day before. By challenges, I am not referring to the rituals of daily life: getting the kids to school on time, juggling work, making phone calls, attending meetings, and still finding time to make dinner. I am talking about deeper challenges that allow us to look back at ourselves down the road with a sense of appreciation and accomplishment, knowing that we are in a better position now than we were then. In this chapter, I hope to help give you ideas on how to cultivate a love for challenge so that if you find yourself in a rut you can liberate yourself.

So where to begin? As with most things, it's not a bad idea to start small. One of the challenges I feel most strongly about, however, is the need to challenge our minds. One of the reasons I feel this way is that while at work in the emergency room, we frequently obtain CT imaging of a patient's head. This is usually in the setting of trauma, or when grandpa just isn't "acting right." Interestingly, when we perform these tests on young or middle-aged people, all too often we will see the radiologist make a comment along the lines of: "Loss of gray matter more advanced than expected for patient's stated age." Translation: this brain appears a lot older than it should. Frequently, this is in the setting of a patient who has a history of drug or alcohol abuse, but not always. What this means is that our brains, just like our muscles, atrophy with disuse. "Use it or lose it," as the saying goes, is definitely true for our brain—our most vital organ.

Why does this happen? Simply put, we have stopped challenging ourselves. Most of us spend the early part of our lives continuously learning, whether it is in formal schooling, or learning new skills at work. However, at some point usually in our twenties or thirties, we have learned virtually all we *need* to know to survive and earn our livings.

At this point, learning, for many people, essentially stops. We get into our routines, living on autopilot through our days; we go home to mindlessly plop down in front of our televisions only to repeat the ritual tomorrow. Our brains, instead of being stimulated to form new neuronal connections, start to wither and eventually atrophy— they are not needed anymore. This makes sense because our brains consume a lot of energy. So, from a survival perspective, we are designed to eliminate any unnecessary baggage.

> *I find that the harder I work,*
> *the more luck I seem to have.*
> —Thomas Jefferson

Why pay, in the form of expended energy, to keep certain cells alive if their function is no longer needed? Unfortunately, the problem is that after these brain cells die, they never come back again. In order to avoid the perpetual collapse into atrophy and cell death, we must strive to keep our neurons alive by frequent stimulation. Fortunately, this is very easy to do, especially in our digital age. The key is to challenge yourself. Grab a newspaper and work through the crossword puzzle or the word jumble. On a more routine level, challenge yourself by taking a new route to work. Our brains crave novelty, so better yet, try to navigate about your city or town without the crutch of turn-by-turn directions from GPS. At work, try learning new skills or ask for a novel assignment. Learn how to do someone else's job or to spearhead a new project. Anything that gets you out of your comfort zone will keep your neurons sharp and healthy.

Thanks to the Internet, learning new things is more accessible than ever. If you have any interests or hobbies at all, I am sure there is a website, blog, or YouTube channel out there that can foster your curiosity. There are even apps on our phones that can help promote brain health. Whether it's a crossword app, or chess, or sudoku, there are plenty of ways to exercise our brains.

Personally, I am a fan of an app called Lumosity, which creates a set of puzzles for you each day that takes less than ten minutes to complete. (Disclosure: I do not receive any financial benefit from Lumosity.) I like this app because it has a variety of types of puzzles, from math challenges to word problems, attention exercises, and spatial recognition problems. You never know what you are going to get each day, so I find this app a great way to keep you on your toes and something you can take with you anywhere. I am sure there are similar apps out there, so check those out too, but again the point is to make your brain work each day.

Reading is a tried-and-true method of nourishing our brains. Unfortunately, as we get into the hectic rat race of adult living, time for reading often falls by the wayside. So, make it a point to read, or better yet make it non-negotiable, as I like to say.

Reading forces our brains to think and imagine. We have to take the words on the page and create an image in our minds, whereas TV does that for us. Furthermore, we have to string together the words to create a cogent idea that the author is trying to convey. Using our imaginations to paint a picture with the words on the page is incredibly challenging and is exactly the stimulation our brains crave.

By reading, we are transported into the author's world, and the ideas they are trying to convey in turn trigger us to expound and dissect those ideas, until we make them our own. This is hard work, which is why many people find that reading makes them sleepy. To get a bonus benefit from reading, use your phone or keep a dictionary nearby to look up any unfamiliar words. You will better understand what the author is trying to say, while expanding your vocabulary at the same time. Does it get any better than that?

I think we have already beat the proverbial horse to death when it comes to exercise, but did you know exercise is also important for brain health? Exercise improves our cardiovascular health, which keeps our blood pressure in check and prevents disease to our arteries including the ones that go to our brains, thereby preventing devastating conditions such as stroke. Better yet, exercise can also be used as a way to challenge our brains. Activities such as strength training, yoga, and cardio exercise improve our sense of balance and coordination, functions that are controlled by the brain.

Furthermore, by introducing a variety of activities into our workouts, such as by running or walking along a new route or doing a different workout regimen each day, we force our brains to learn new things. This prevents atrophy. But I mention this only in case you didn't already understand the importance of exercise from our earlier discussion.

Let me stress: One of the most obvious ways to nourish our brains is by learning something new. It is now easier than ever to learn a new language, whether by watching YouTube or using a free app like Duolingo. There are also other online courses and paid applications. There might even be a Meetup group in your area where you can practice the language and meet people with similar interests at the same time.

How about those who have always wanted to learn to play an instrument? Well, the Internet has you covered there as well. What a great way to challenge yourself while learning something you can feel good about both as a stress reliever and a way to feel like you're improving yourself. Another bonus: learn to play a song on your favorite instrument and sing it in the new language you are learning. Now that is impressive!

Okay, so maybe new languages aren't for you, and you're not interested in music; there are still many practical ways to challenge ourselves. If you own a home, why don't you learn how to do some repairs yourself? If something breaks down rather than calling in a local expert for help, at least try to figure it out yourself, even if ultimately you need help repairing it. Try to diagnose the problem yourself, and perhaps you might realize that it's a simpler fix than you thought. Thanks to Google and YouTube, chances are you can probably find a forum or a video of people who have had similar problems, who will give you ideas on how to make a repair. Not only will this stimulate your brain, but you will be better prepared to understand what is causing the problem. Knowledge truly is power.

Hopefully by now you get the idea, and I have motivated you to start challenging yourself to break out of your comfort zone. Whether it's a new language, a new skill, a larger vocabulary, or changing your role at work, challenging yourself in this way will allow you to look back at yourself weeks and months from now and know that you have improved from where you were before. Our brains and our bodies seek novelty, challenge, and stimulation, so give them what they want. You will reap the benefits in terms of a longer, healthier, and more satisfying life.

# In Conclusion

*I wish you were either cold or hot.*
—Revelations 3:15

I find it fitting that I end the book with a quote from the last book of the Christian Bible. Let me be clear that this book is not meant to push any one religion. Instead, I merely chose this passage because my Catholic background is a part of me, and I wish to share with you a poignant passage that I read many years ago. I imagine there are other religions or philosophers who echo similar sentiments, but this passage has stuck with me and I believe is a perfect way to conclude.

In short, the passage refers to living our lives actively and full of passion. The Bible is referring to the notion that God does not want us to be lukewarm in our love toward Him, but we can extrapolate that idea into the totality of our lives. I mean, simply reflecting on a literal interpretation of the passage instantly gives insight into what the author of the passage is saying.

Think about it, what in your life do you prefer to be lukewarm? A cup of soup? No, either you want a piping hot cup of bisque or a cool and refreshing gazpacho. Who wants to relax in a lukewarm bath or a tepid "hot" tub? Who likes their beer to be room temperature? Okay, maybe the Brits, but they also spell color with a "u," so we can't go by them. All jokes aside, a quick inventory will demonstrate that we much prefer things to be one

164

or the other, black or white. Even in our politics, is it the moderate liberals or the milquetoast conservatives who get the spotlight? No, it's the firebrands on either side. Similarly, this is what God in this Bible passage is exhorting us to do, almost as if He knows human nature better than ourselves.

Similarly, I encourage you to be hot or cold in your life, or to put it more succinctly: be decisive. Resolve to commit to goals. When it comes to friends and family, don't be a flake. If you say you are going to be somewhere, show up. Don't back out at the last minute. If you say you are going to do something, do it. Don't make excuses. If there is a conflict in your life, or an issue to be resolved, pick a side or take a stand. You don't have to make decisions hastily. In fact, the more complex the issue, the more time you should take, but don't allow yourself to be wishy-washy or in limbo on issues in of real value to you. And, being decisive does not mean you cannot change your mind or admit you were wrong should new evidence arise or situations change.

Of course, most issues in the world are not black and white, and many situations are shades of gray. However, we should avoid living "gray" lives ourselves. Explore what your principles are and stand by them, lest you be accused of being a hypocrite, doing one thing one day and another the next day. By becoming keenly aware of your principles and what is important to you, you can use these principles to guide your decisions and actions. You want to be someone with whom people know where they stand and can predict how you are going to react based on the principles you've demonstrated in your life. You do not want to be volatile, emotionally unstable, or worse, a so-called pushover. Being borderline may land you a starring role on *Investigation Discovery* or other crime shows, but it is not the foundation for solid relationships.

I am not advocating that we need to be rigid or inflexible. Nor am I saying that we need to lump everything into buckets of "good" and "bad," and there are times when we need to be tolerant, patient, and open-minded. On the whole, we should strive to be decisive in our philosophy as well as our short- and long-term goals. Ambivalence is a key ingredient for anxiety. Those who have suffered from anxiety or panic should know exactly what I am talking about. When you are in the midst of a panic attack, you are figuratively paralyzed. You feel you are being pulled in multiple directions at once, but unable to go toward any one of them. It's terrifying. One way to avoid ending up in the throes of a panic attack is to practice living decisively.

*I would rather die of passion than of boredom.*
—Vincent van Gogh

We live in a world of such choice and abundance that it can be crippling. Failure to be decisive in such a world can lead to constant decision paralysis, where even choosing a brand of deodorant, let alone our college majors, can seem to be an insurmountable choice. When making plans for an evening out has never before have we had such an abundance of choice, be it choosing a restaurant or an entertainment activity. All these choices can certainly lead to anxiety in what popular culture refers to as FOMO (fear of missing out). Economists call this opportunity cost, which means that when we make one decision we invariably need to give up some other option.

For example, our work friends Kimmy and Will are having parties the same night (and assuming it's not possible to go to both); if we go to Kimmy's party we will miss out on Will's party, and vice versa. Maybe Kimmy will serve better food, but Will's parties always end up being a wild night. Consequently, we might get a sense of FOMO when we ruminate about the opportunity costs of attending either party. On Monday at the office will everyone be talking about Will's wild party, or will they be going on about Kimmy's crab puffs? Oh, which party to choose....

Here is where living life hot or cold comes into play. The key to avoiding FOMO and its resulting anxiety is to make a decision and stick with it. Be decisive. Pick a party and stick to it, and don't even think about the other party as being a possibility. (Of course, send a polite note of declination to whomever's party you do not attend. We are not savages here!) Then, be present when you attend the party and enjoy yourself. Regardless of which event you decided to attend, be mindfully present both out of respect to your host and yourself. If you find yourself wondering what the other party is like or what you must be "missing out on," simply draw your mind back into the present and focus on enjoying yourself. You made a decision, now stick with it. Your life will be so much better if you are not perpetually wondering *what if....*

Being decisive is so important for our relationships, even from an early age. Research in a field of psychology called *attachment theory* demonstrates that we form secure attachments with our parents when boundaries are clear and decisive. For instance, when parents are present in the lives of their children, the rules are well-defined, and love is not conditional. These children have been shown to tolerate loss and separation better than kids with more chaotic upbringings. In one particular study, kids who had more secure relationships with their parents were shown to cry less often and for shorter amounts of time when separated from their parents compared to kids with less secure attachments. These traits carry forward as these children become adults; they are able to maintain more secure relationships with others. They are less anxious, less jealous, and more stable in their friendships and romances. This is called *secure attachment.*

Imagine instead environments in which children are raised in a household where rules are more gray rather than black and white. A child who was not given any rules, who never knew when or if their parents were coming home, is exposed to a more chaotic upbringing. This can lead to what is termed an *anxious attachment*, and understandably so. These children are likely to grow into adults who are always afraid that important people will leave them, or, they have difficulty when it comes to making big choices in life, never knowing a sense of stability or having a firm foundation. Kids crave security and a sense of order (even if they tell you they only crave candy and ice cream).

This is a theory, and there are always caveats and corollaries to theories. Moreover, there are cases of children being raised in chaotic environments who become well-adjusted and successful adults. There are also kids with very solid upbringings who go on to live chaotic and disorderly adult lives. However, in general, being raised in a setting where the rules are clearly defined, and where a child knows what to expect, is more likely to foster secure attachment styles in children. As a result, it is vitally important for both ourselves and our children that we are clear and decisive.

People mistakenly think that being decisive closes us off from opportunities, and that it is better to leave all possibilities open. Although I don't believe in prematurely closing doors, I think that we should mentally explore all options, but failing to commit is a recipe for disaster. Take romantic relationships for instance. There is wisdom in making the decision to marry someone, to say that you want to spend the rest of your life with them. Again, there may be exceptions, but most people want stability in their relationships.

They want to know that each partner is the other's one and only. If you are dating someone for a while, and you don't see marriage or some other form of commitment in your future, it is time to be hot or cold. You are not doing yourself or your current partner any favors by staying in a lukewarm relationship just because it's familiar. You may think you are keeping your options open, but in fact you are closing yourself off to the benefits of a decisively committed and devoted relationship that marriage brings.

The importance of being hot or cold applies to every aspect of our lives. The more we can be "all-in" on our decisions the easier life becomes. Committing to decisions in our lives liberates us from the anxiety that comes with having a plan B. For instance, let's say you want to be a Broadway actress. You are far more likely to be successful if you tirelessly go to auditions, starting in smaller parts or productions off Broadway, all the while pursuing singing and acting classes and working each day to get closer to your dream. You are far less likely to be successful if you are lukewarm about pursuing acting. Maybe you attend an audition or two, or a class here and there, but in the back of your mind you know it's a long shot and you figure you will just fall back on being a teacher or an accountant or something more practical anyway. Being lukewarm becomes a self-fulfilling prophecy, and your plan B or C actually prevents you from achieving your plan A. So, make a decision for what you want in your life and go all in.

Before drawing this book to a close, I would like to mention one more way in which being lukewarm pervades our lives, and that is with regard to our language. What I am referring is to the seemingly ubiquitous use of qualifiers in our speech. Words and phrases such as "like," "sort of," "kind of," and "maybe" have infiltrated our language and culture. These words reflect a plague of indecision in our lives. As an example, I remember being a resident and telling a particularly ornery attending physician of mine that the patient I had just examined was "kind of wheezing." He looked at me and point-blank said, "I have no idea what that means." Sheepishly, I knew he was right—I was being wishy-washy, failing to commit, and not confident in my exam or my own judgment as a physician. I mean, someone is either wheezing or they aren't. It is a yes or no question.

Ever since that day, I resolved, at least in my medical career, to never hedge in my presentations. I commit to making decisions and letting the chips fall where they may. I am so grateful I have. By making my own decisions I learned far more from my attending physicians than I would have had I simply hedged in my presentations and left the decision-making up to them. After all, in a few short years, I would be the one making the decisions, without a supervising physician to fall back on. I don't think my patients would appreciate it if I told them that they are "kind of gonna live" or their kidneys are "sort of failing." Certainly, they would want a second, more decisive, opinion.

As mentioned, this type of vague language, for myself included, easily pervades our entire lives and ways of thinking. How many times have you said things such as "I sort of like him," "I kind of want to go," or "maybe I'll be there." There is a time and a place for qualifiers such as these in our lives—the world is not always black and white. However, the problem arises when these words become so ingrained in our vernaculars that we are constantly hedging with our thoughts and feelings, and consequently our lives.

Making a conscious effort to at the very least be careful with these words, or better yet, avoid them whenever possible, will allow you to start taking control of your language and better express yourself. After all, people will likely be far more interested in how you actually feel or what you really want to do rather than how you "kind of" feel or what you "sort of" want to do. Being assertive in our language goes a long way toward retaking charge of our lives.

In closing, being hot or cold perfectly summarizes so many of the ideas I have discussed in the preceding chapters in this book. I first started by talking about having a wake-up call, which metaphorically means snapping out of your lukewarm life and getting thrown into the frying pan (or the ice box, if you prefer). It means waking up to the difference between merely existing, versus living and thriving. You stop living a tepid life when you stop lying to yourself and stop comparing yourself to others with a "woe is me" attitude. Only then can you stop shooting yourself in the foot and start making goals and, more importantly, making them non-negotiable.

Living hot or cold means no longer getting trapped in a life that is not heading where you want it to. It means controlling your health, both physical and financial. I hope this book gives you the tools to start ridding yourself of anxiety while focusing on what is best for you and caring less about what other people might think about you.

Hopefully, I have empowered you to think about the relationships in your lives and how to nurture the positive ones and dump the toxic ones. How you deal with relationships is a perfect example of the importance of being either hot or cold: you want to be hot toward the people who are adding to your life and cold to the ones who are detracting. Being mild or cool in these cases can alienate those who want the best for you, while letting those who might not have your best interests in mind continue to smolder in the background.

Remember, living with passion instills a sense of gratitude as you learn to never take a day for granted and to never be halfhearted in your efforts. This gratitude will motivate you to continue to better yourself and seek out new challenges and opportunities, knowing that it is only through struggling that we become a little bit better than we were the day before.

I've covered a lot in this book, and I truly hope you have gained something from the time we have spent together. If there is one thing that you take away from this book, it should be that you are in control of your own destiny. We are all dealt hands in life, but it is up to us to decide if we are going to work to improve those hands, or if we would rather fold and let life do what it may to us. The choice is ours to make, and it is my goal that this book gives you some of the tools you need to embark on the path to self-improvement. So now, it is with great pride and joy that I can definitively tell you that you are ready to stop sabotaging your future and live the live you want!

# About the Author

**Maxwell Morrison, M.D.,** is a practicing emergency medicine physician in the Dallas–Fort Worth metroplex in Texas. He earned his Bachelor of Science degree in Mechanical Engineering with honors from SUNY Binghamton. He studied medicine at SUNY Stony Brook, where he graduated with a Doctor of Medicine in 2012. He was also inducted into Alpha Omega Alpha, the Medical Honor Society.

After medical school, Dr. Morrison pursued his residency training at St. Luke's-Roosevelt Hospital located in the Upper West Side of Manhattan, in association with the Icahn School of Medicine at Mount Sinai Hospital. He graduated in 2015, and moved to Texas, where he has practiced in community emergency rooms.

He is certified with the American Board of Emergency Medicine. He currently serves on the stroke committee at Medical City Lewisville, Texas; he also works on promoting the use of bedside ultrasound technology in clinical practice.

Dr. Morrison was born and raised on Long Island, New York along with five siblings including an identical twin brother. He currently resides with his husband outside of Dallas, Texas. A dog lover, he has a golden doodle, Willy, and a labradoodle, Winston. In his free time, Dr. Morrison enjoys playing with his dogs, reading, playing piano, linguistics, and oenology—the study of wines.

## Consumer Health Titles from Addicus Books
Visit our online catalog at www.AddicusBooks.com

**To Order Books:**
**Visit us online at:** www.AddicusBooks.com
**Call toll-free:** (800) 888-4741

*Addicus Books is dedicated to publishing consumer health books
that comfort and educate.*